Cute Animals
Coloring Book

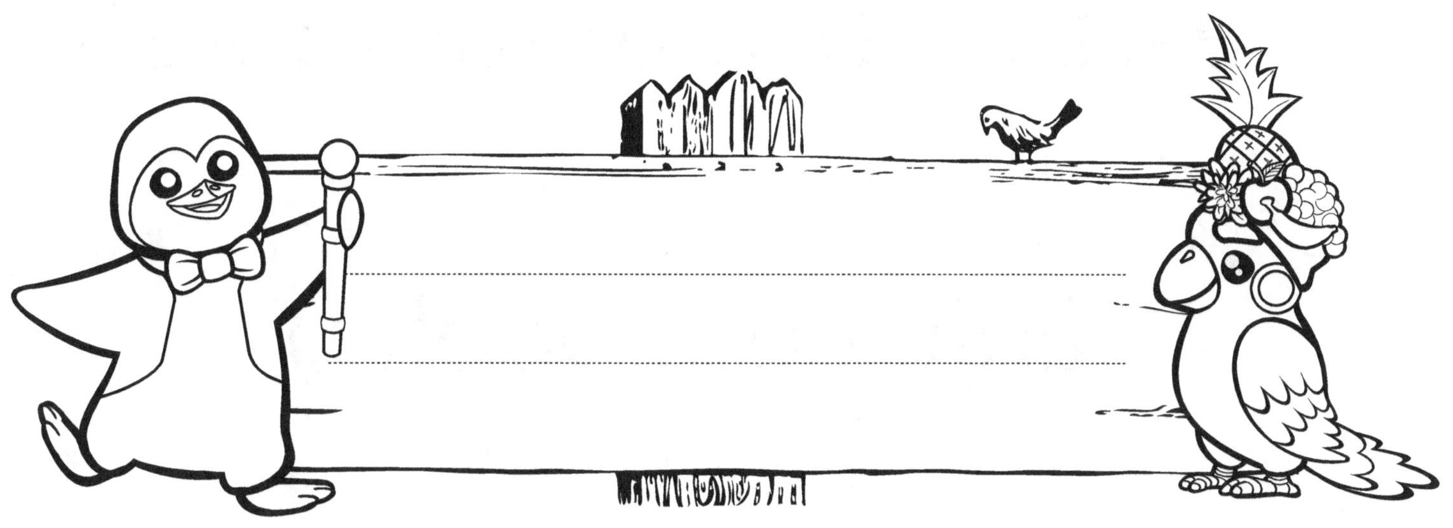

Book Guide

Color the white area

Cut the paper if you like

Paste it on your room wall

Enjoy the book ;)

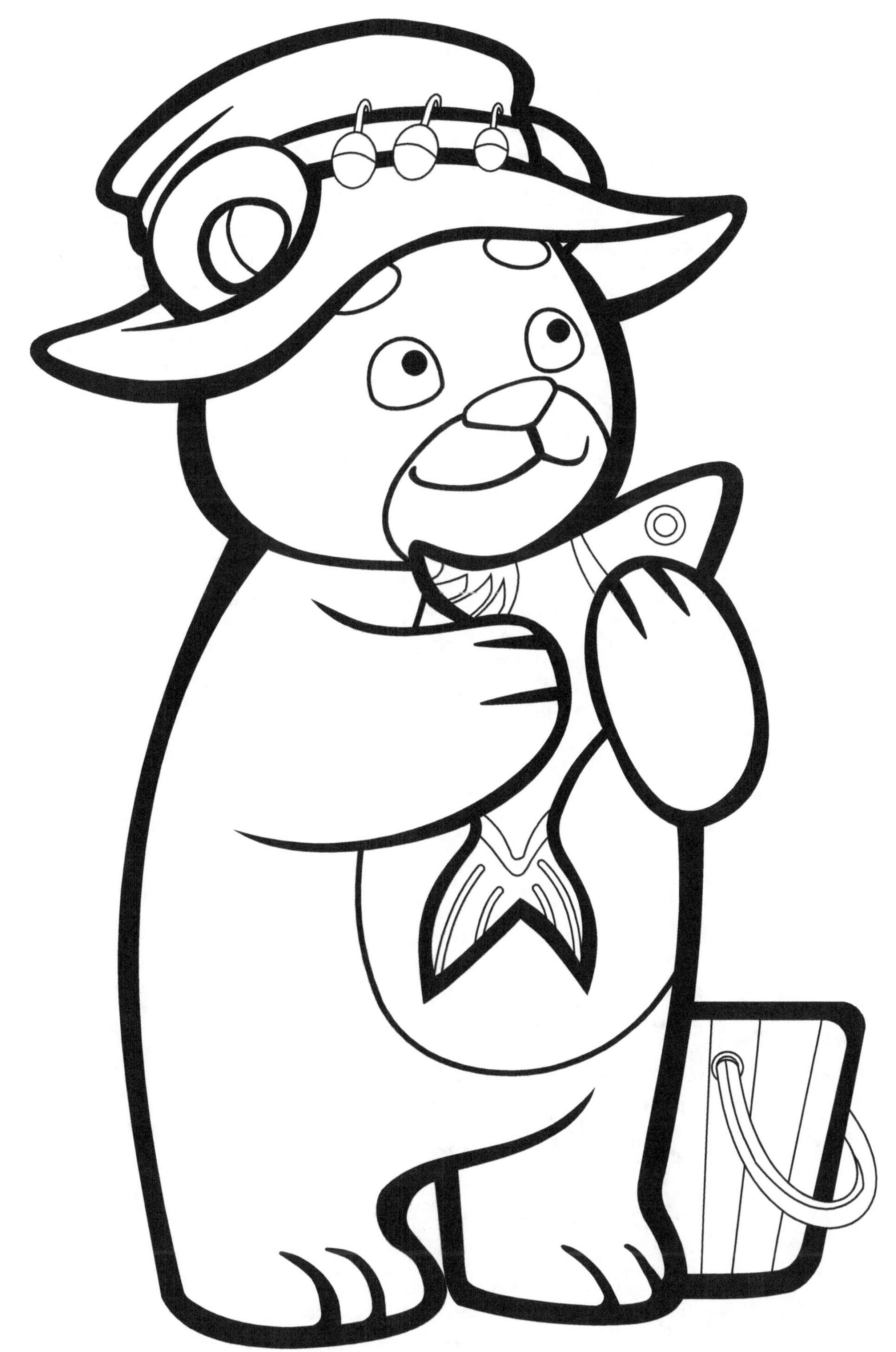

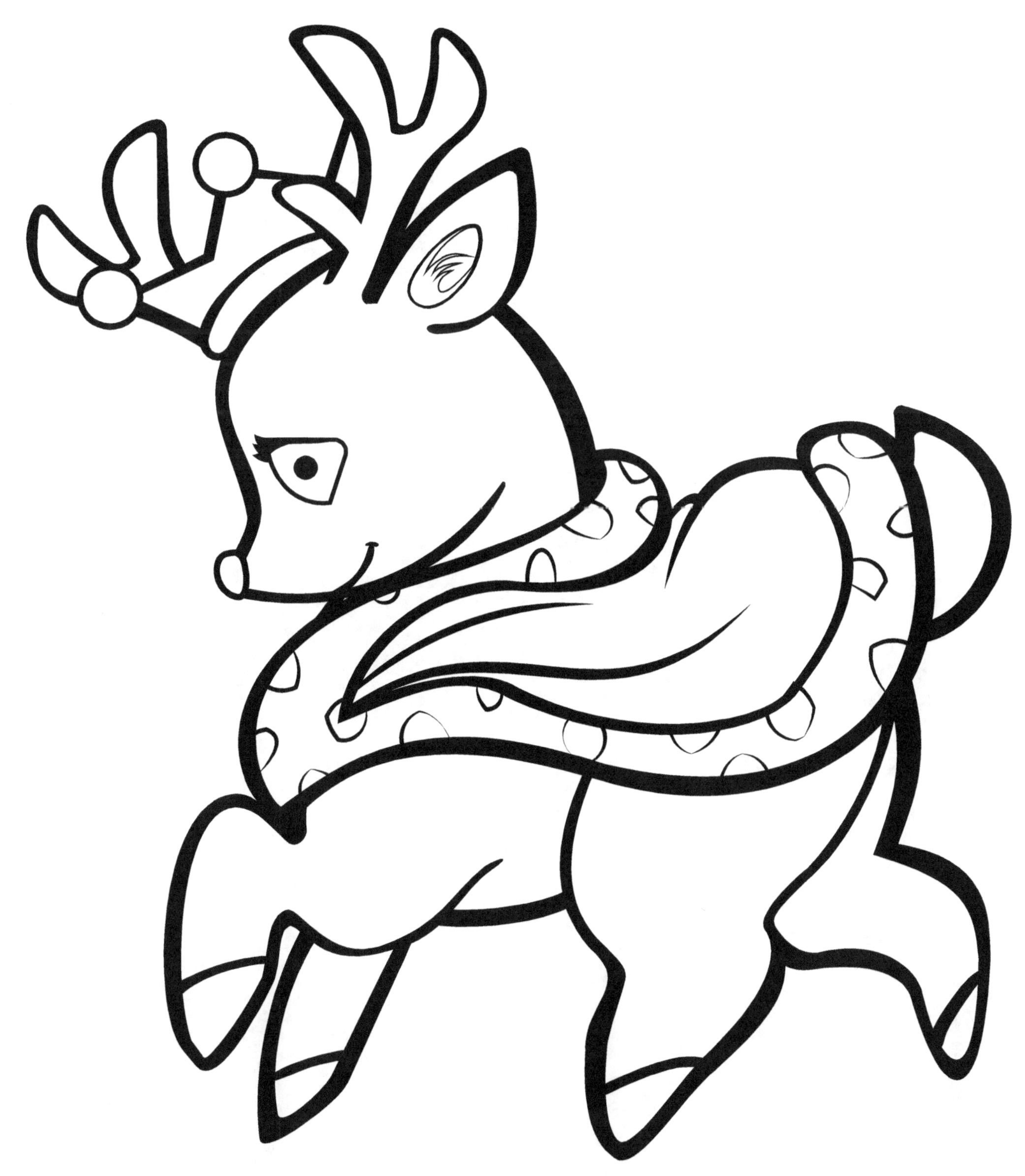

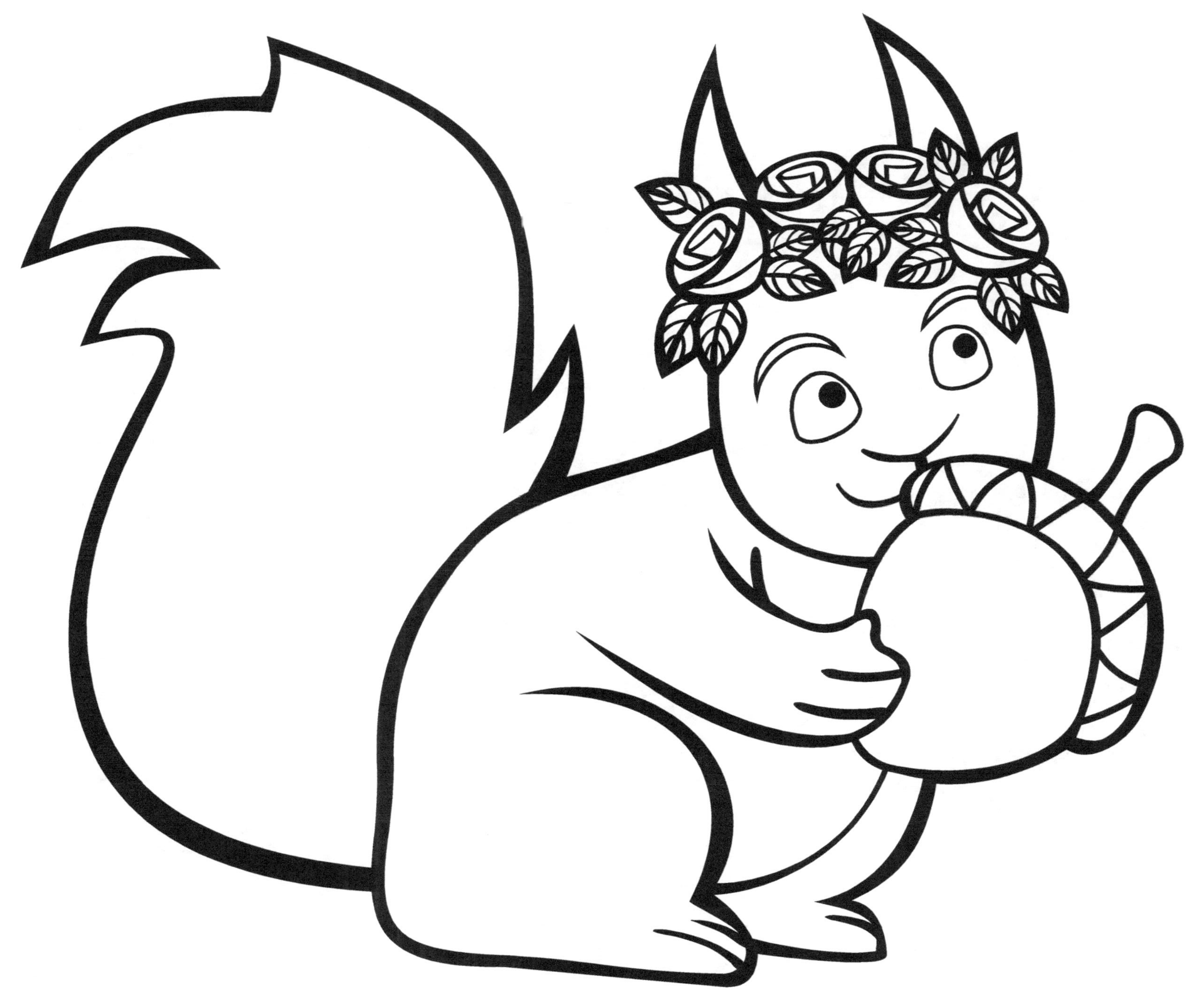

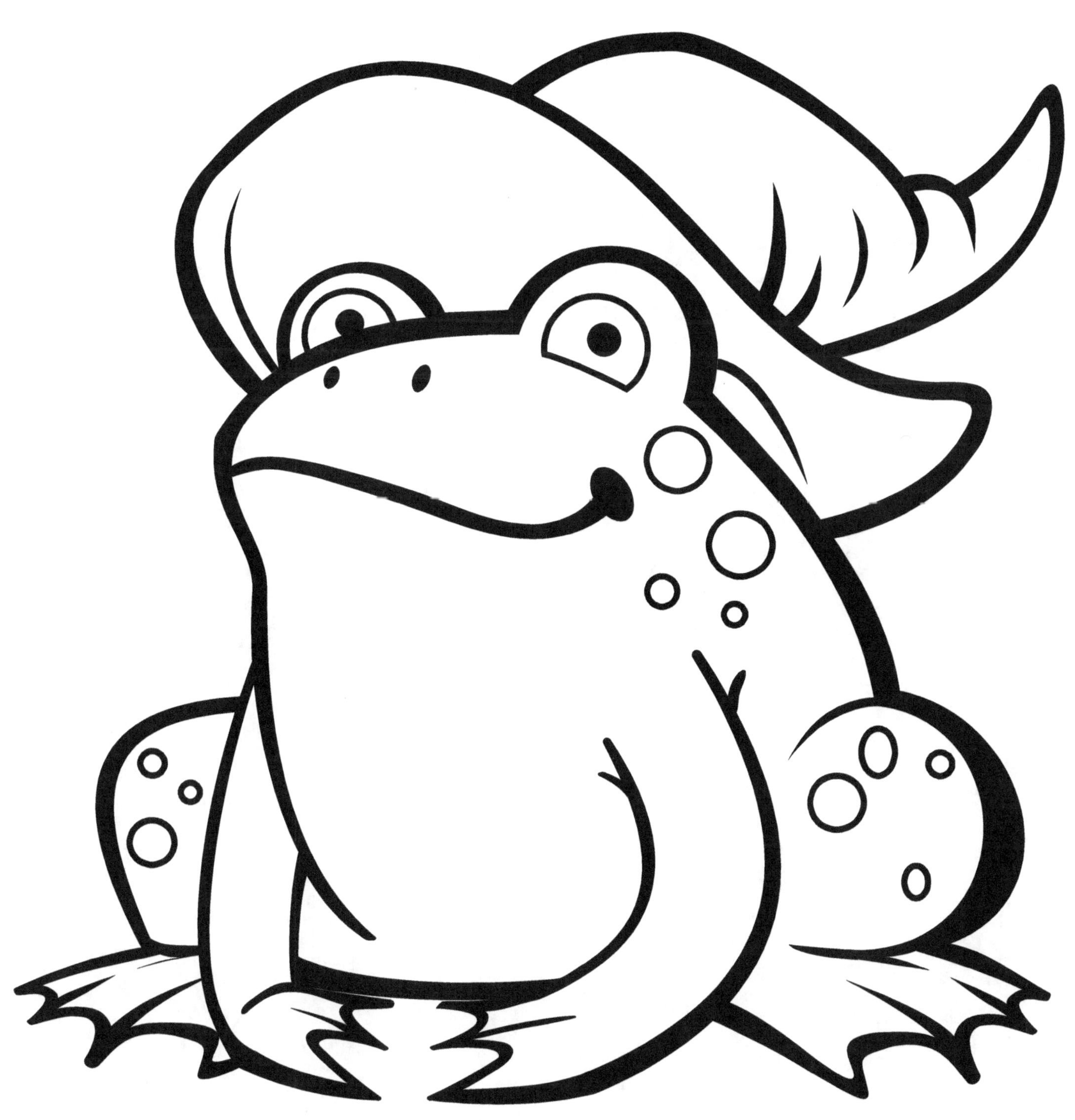

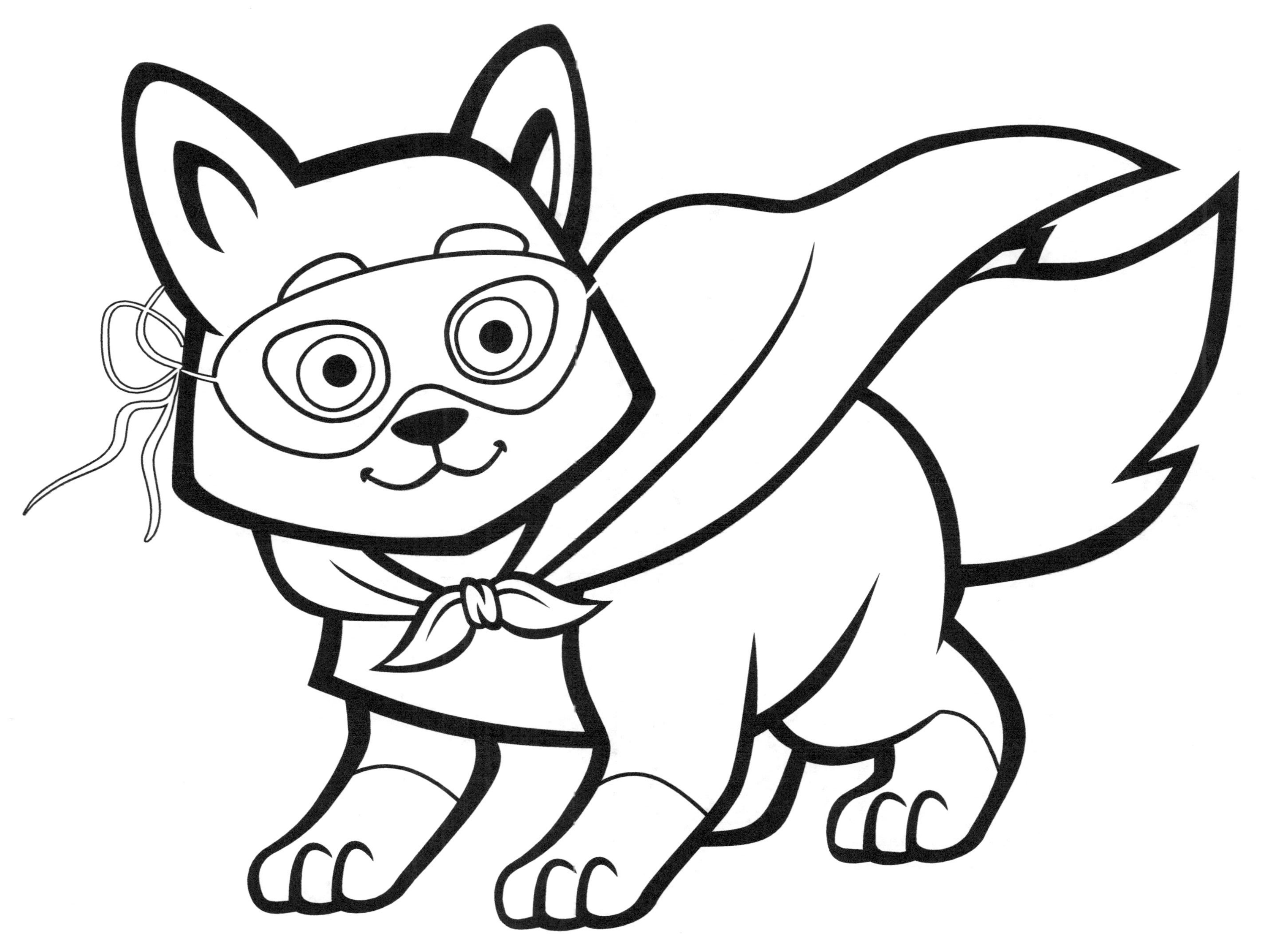

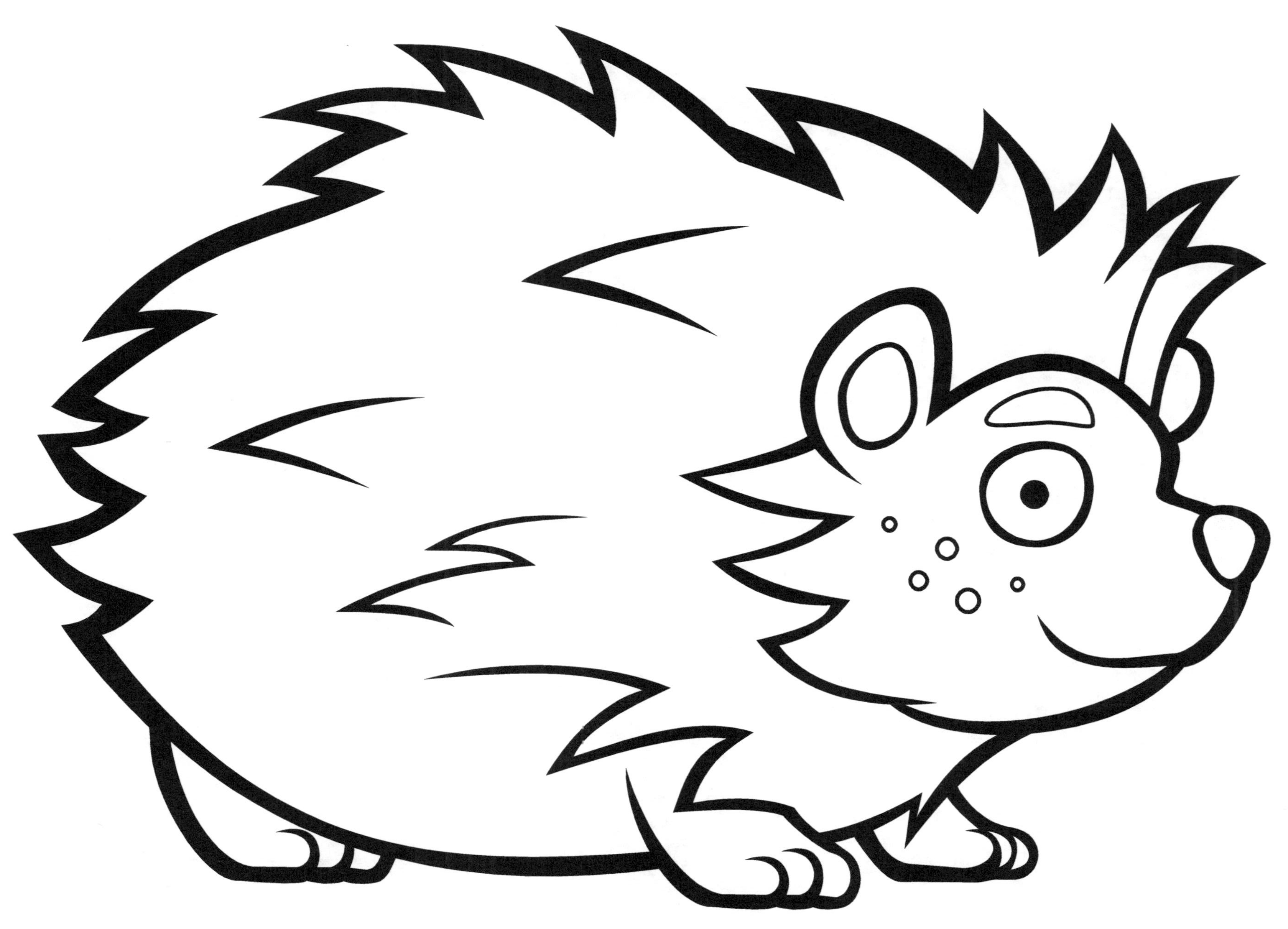

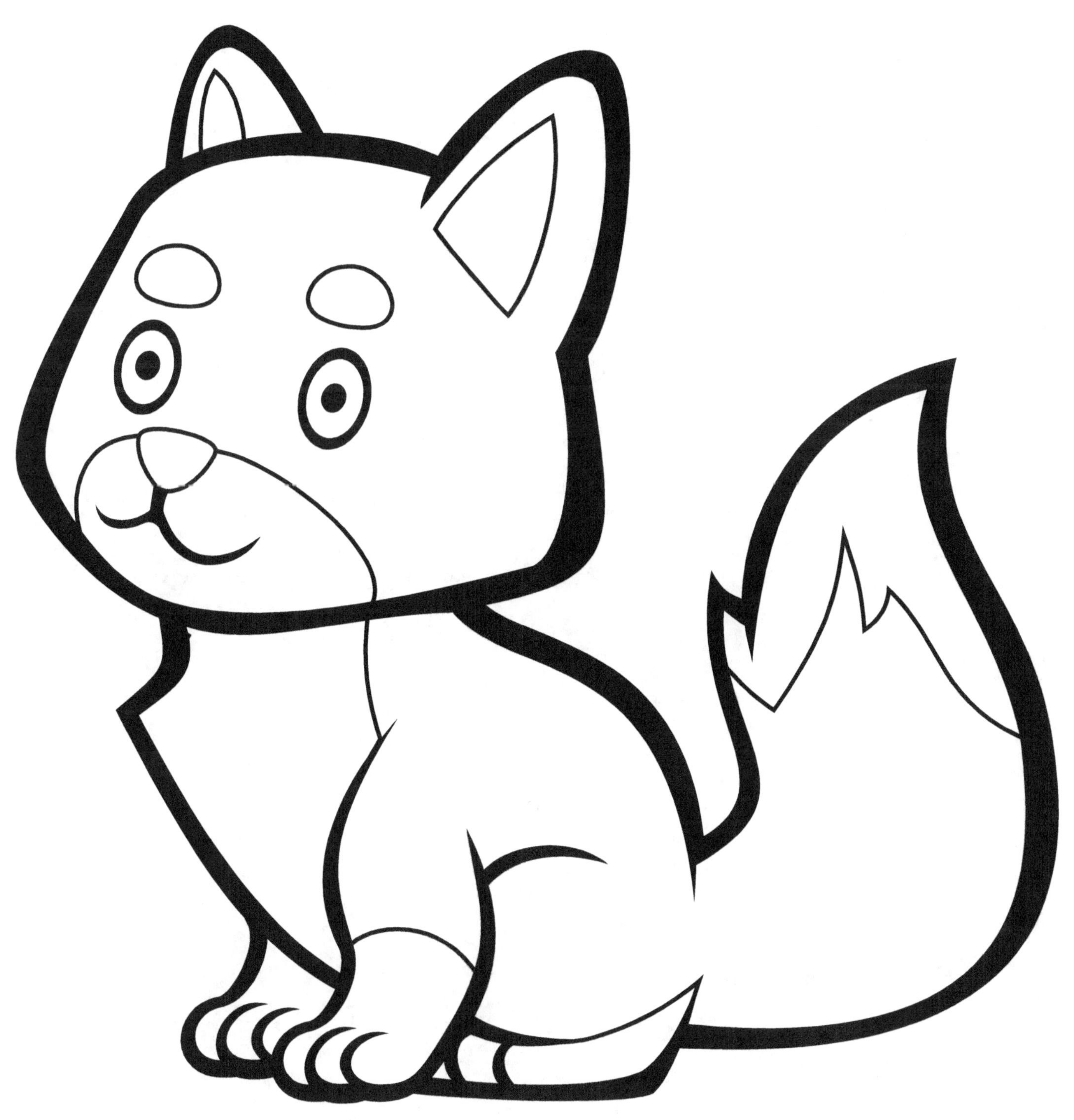

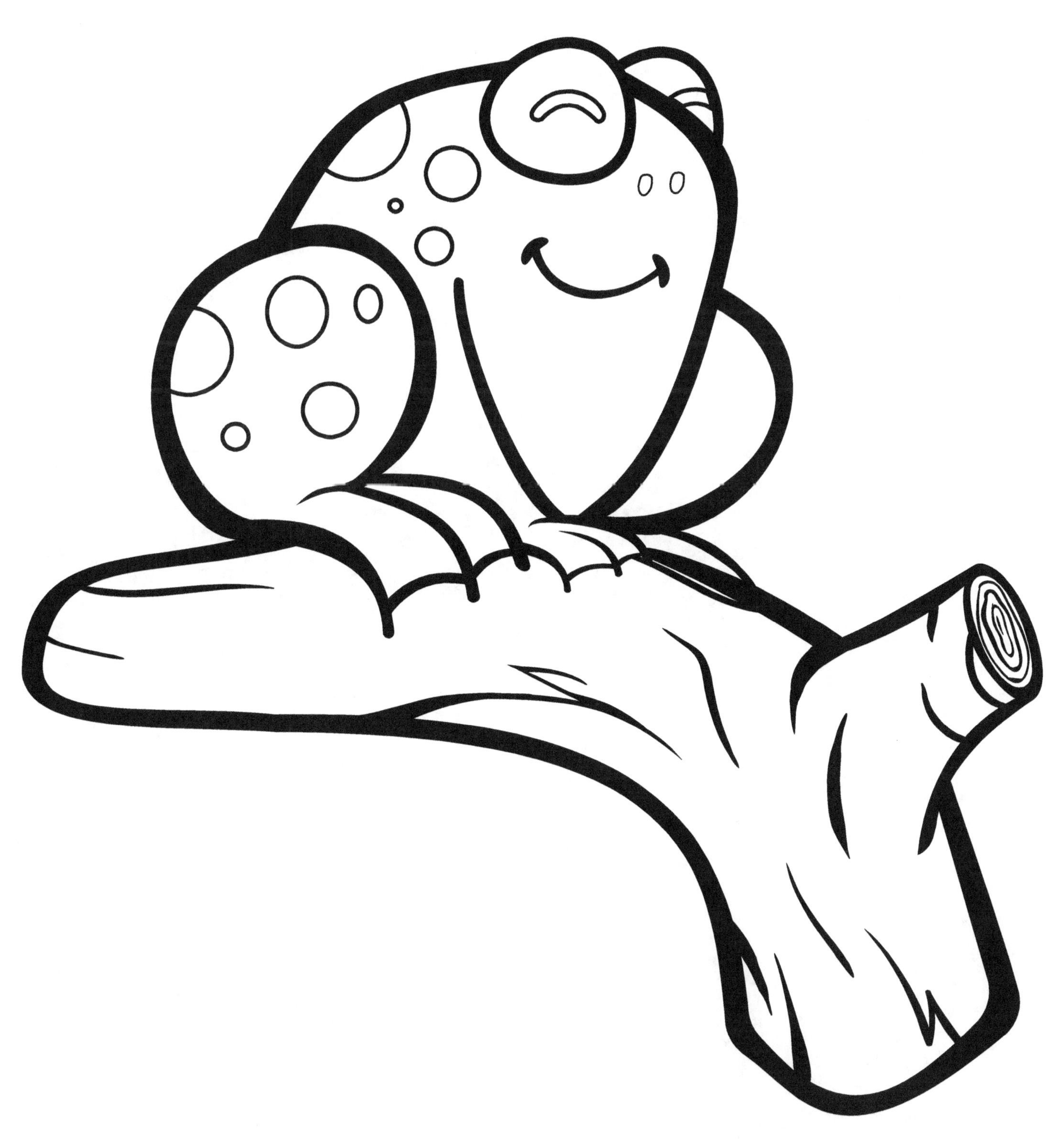

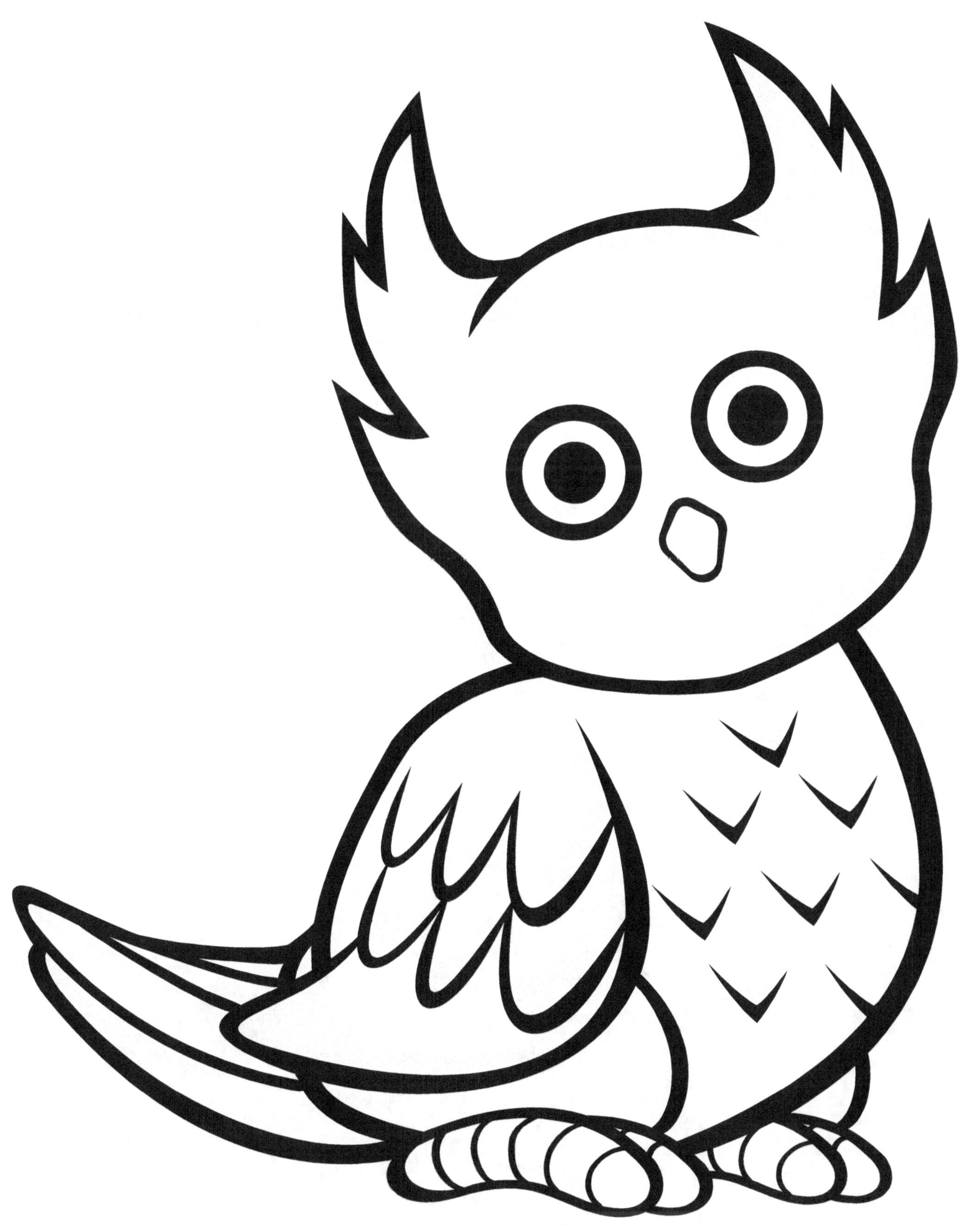

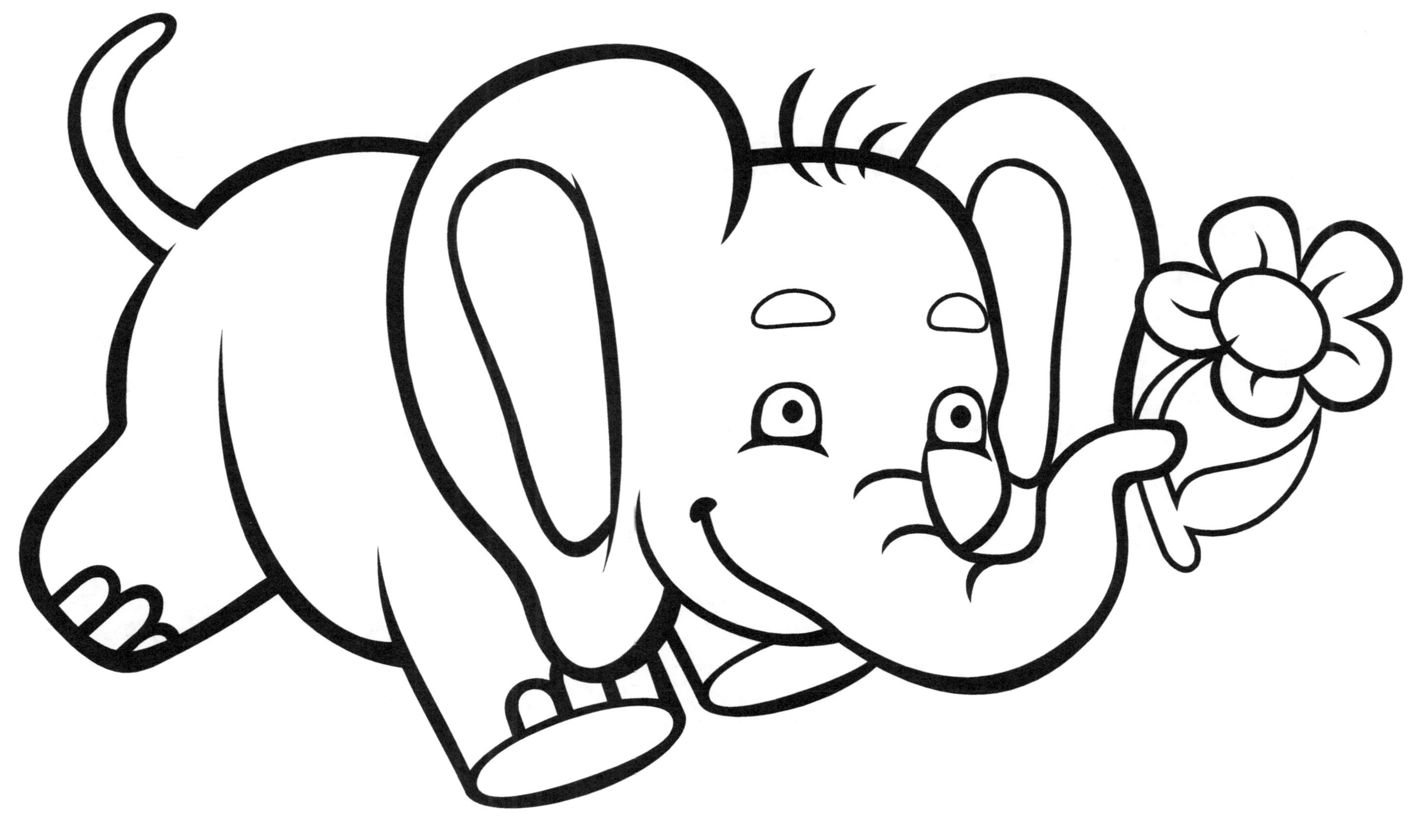

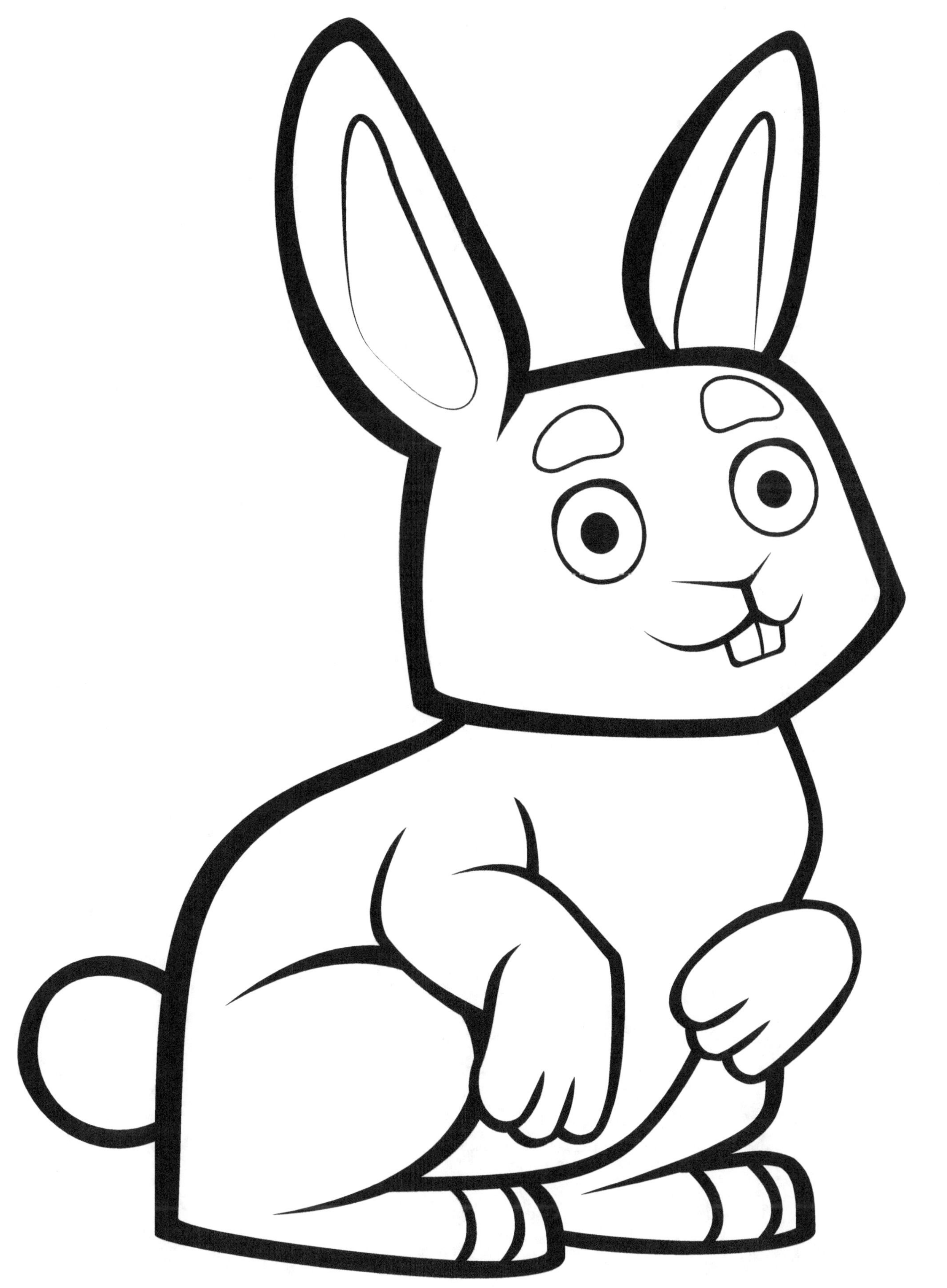

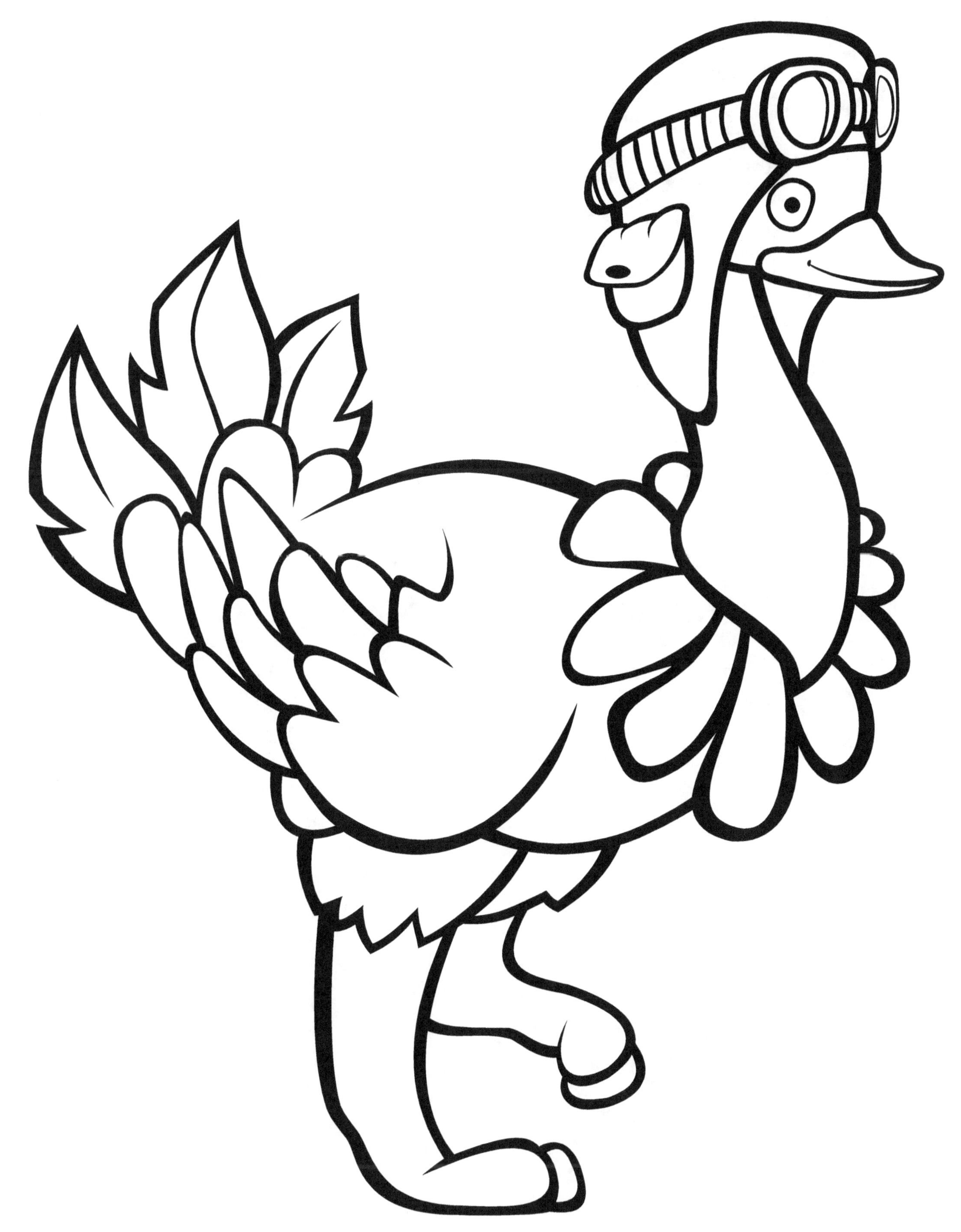

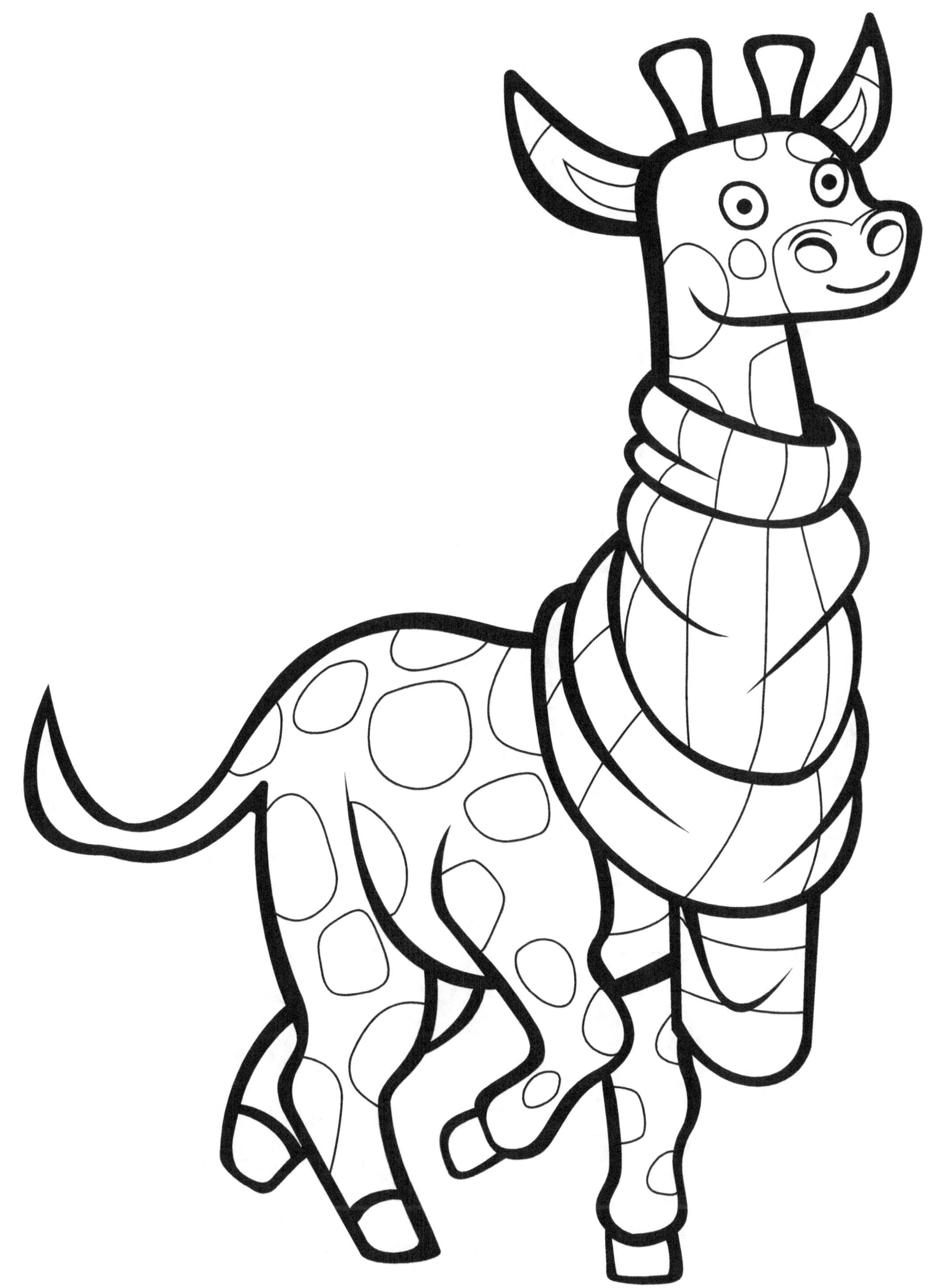

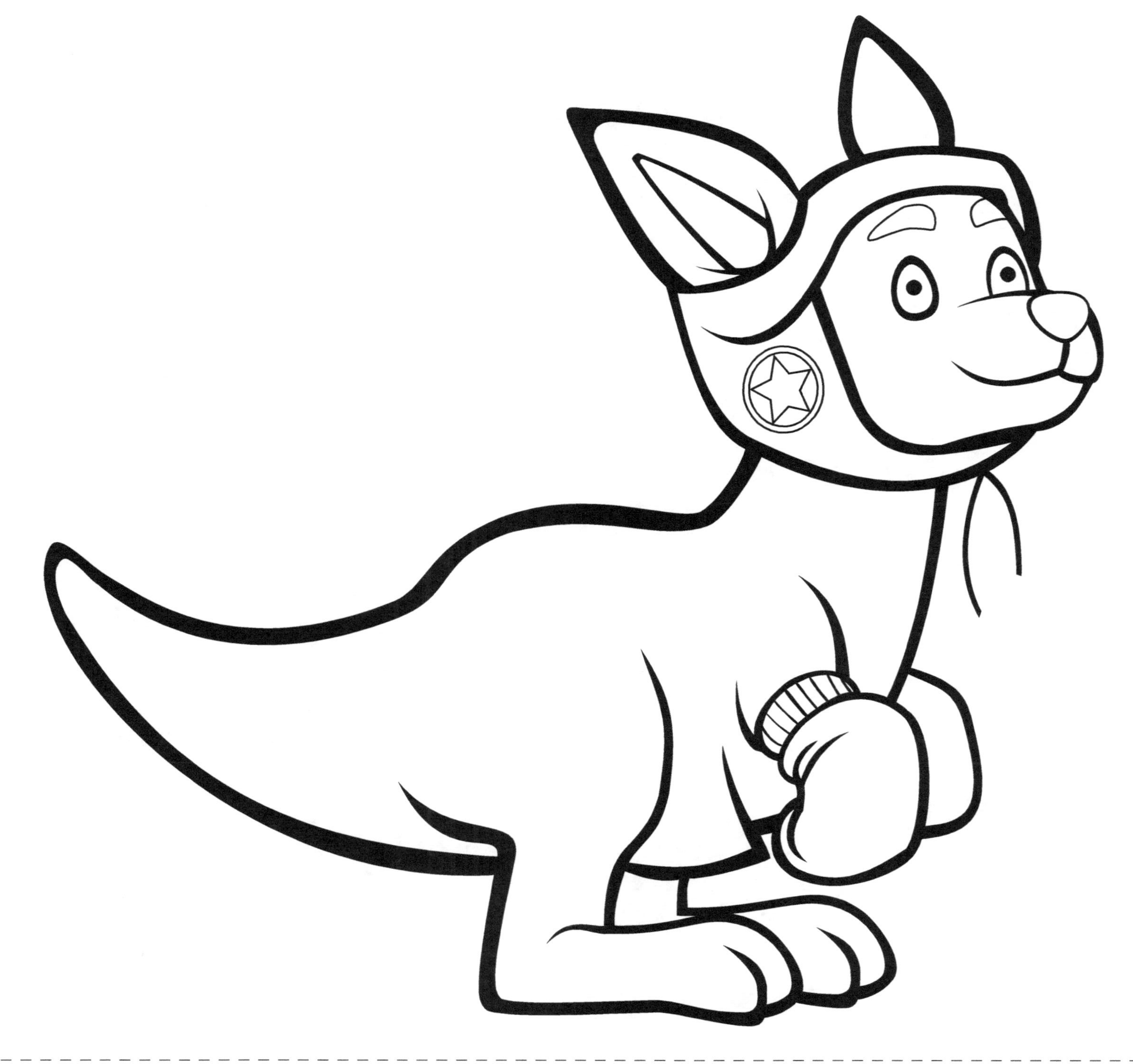

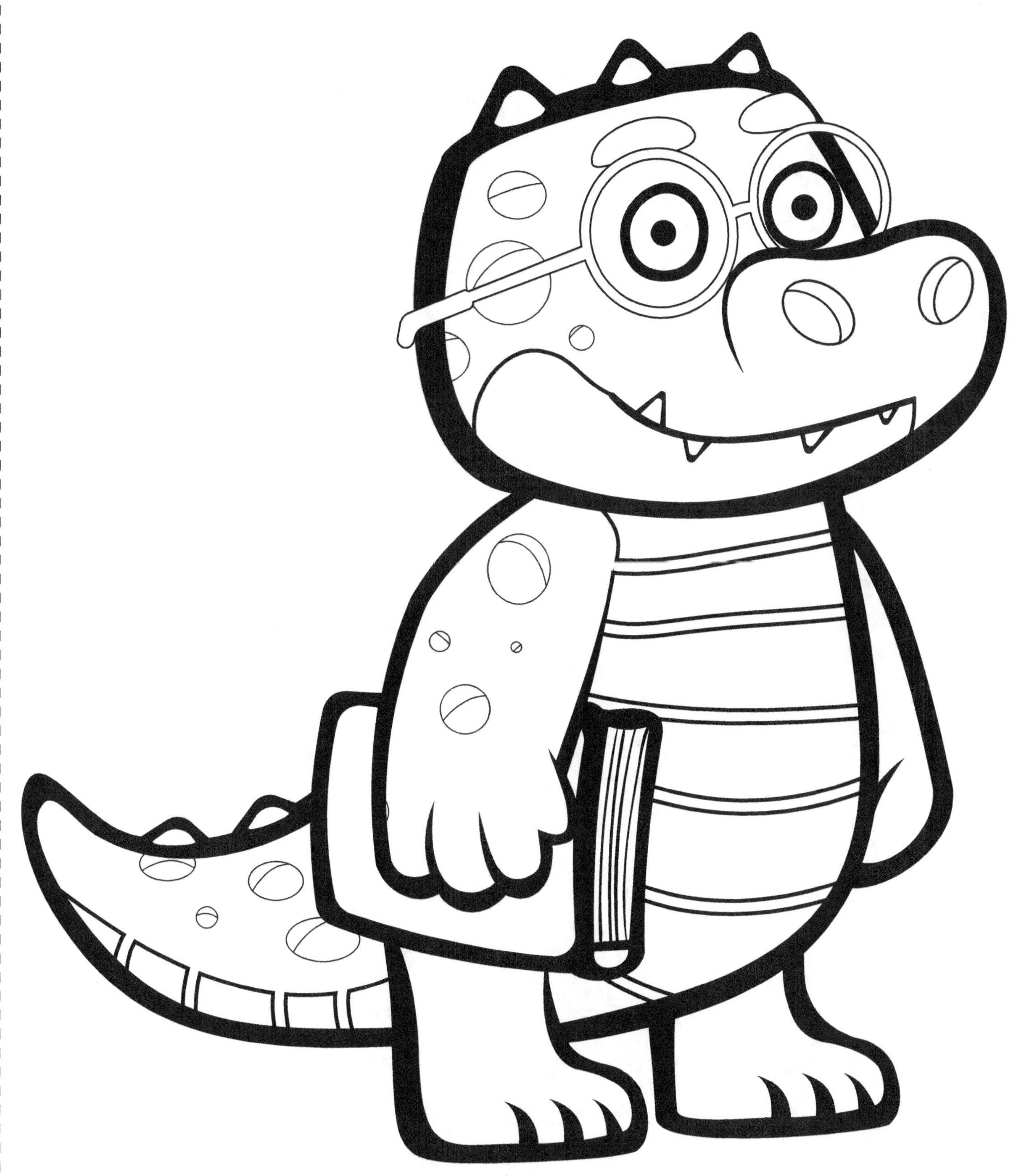

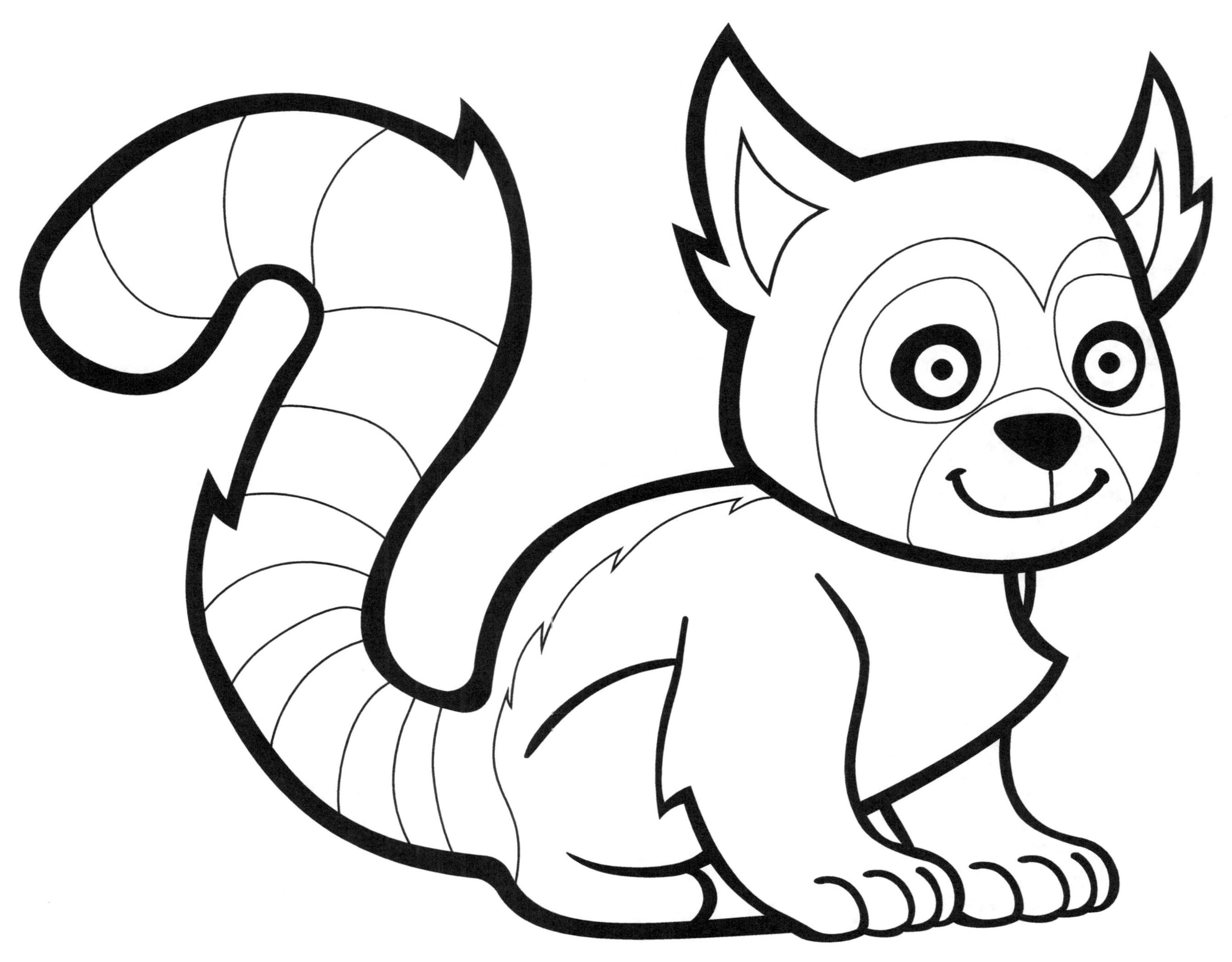

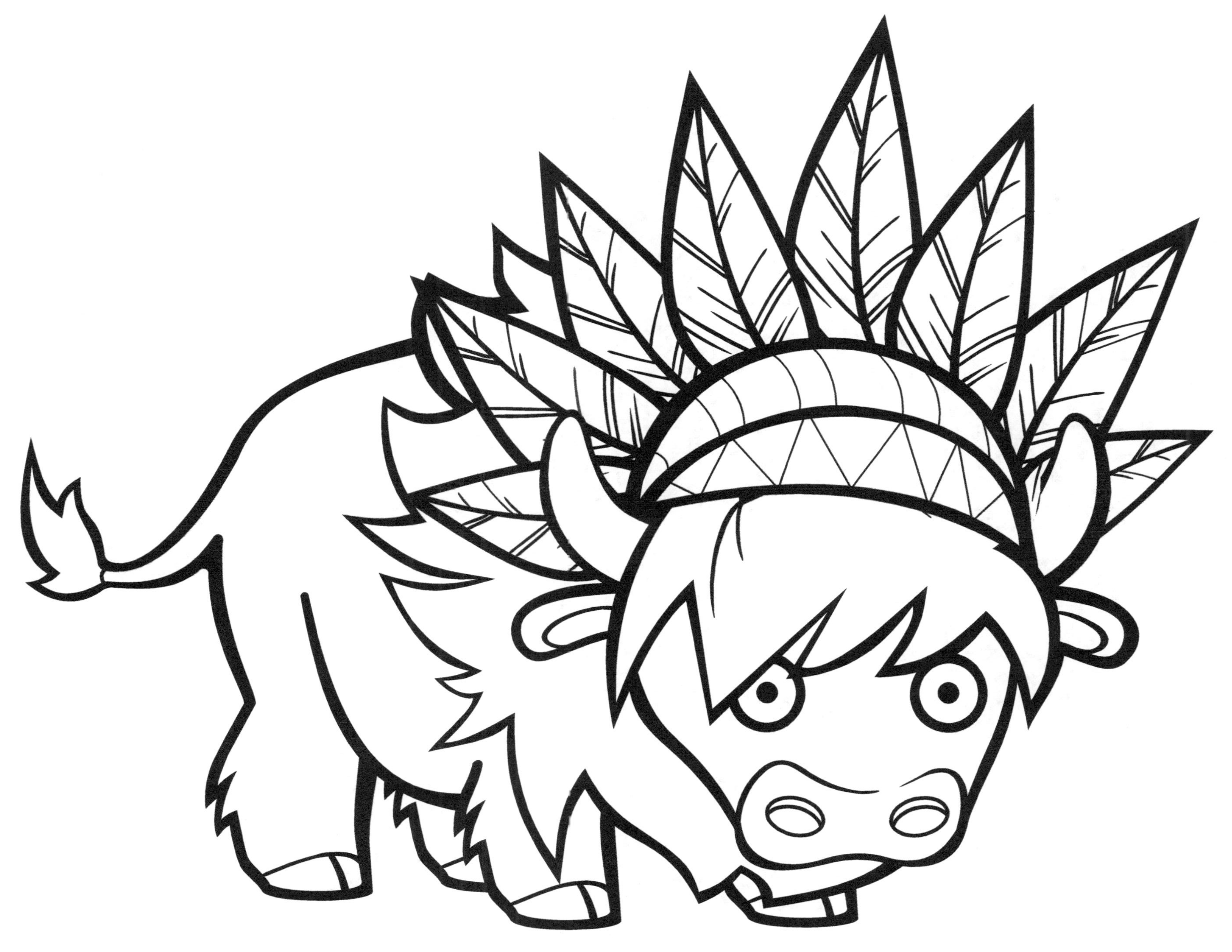

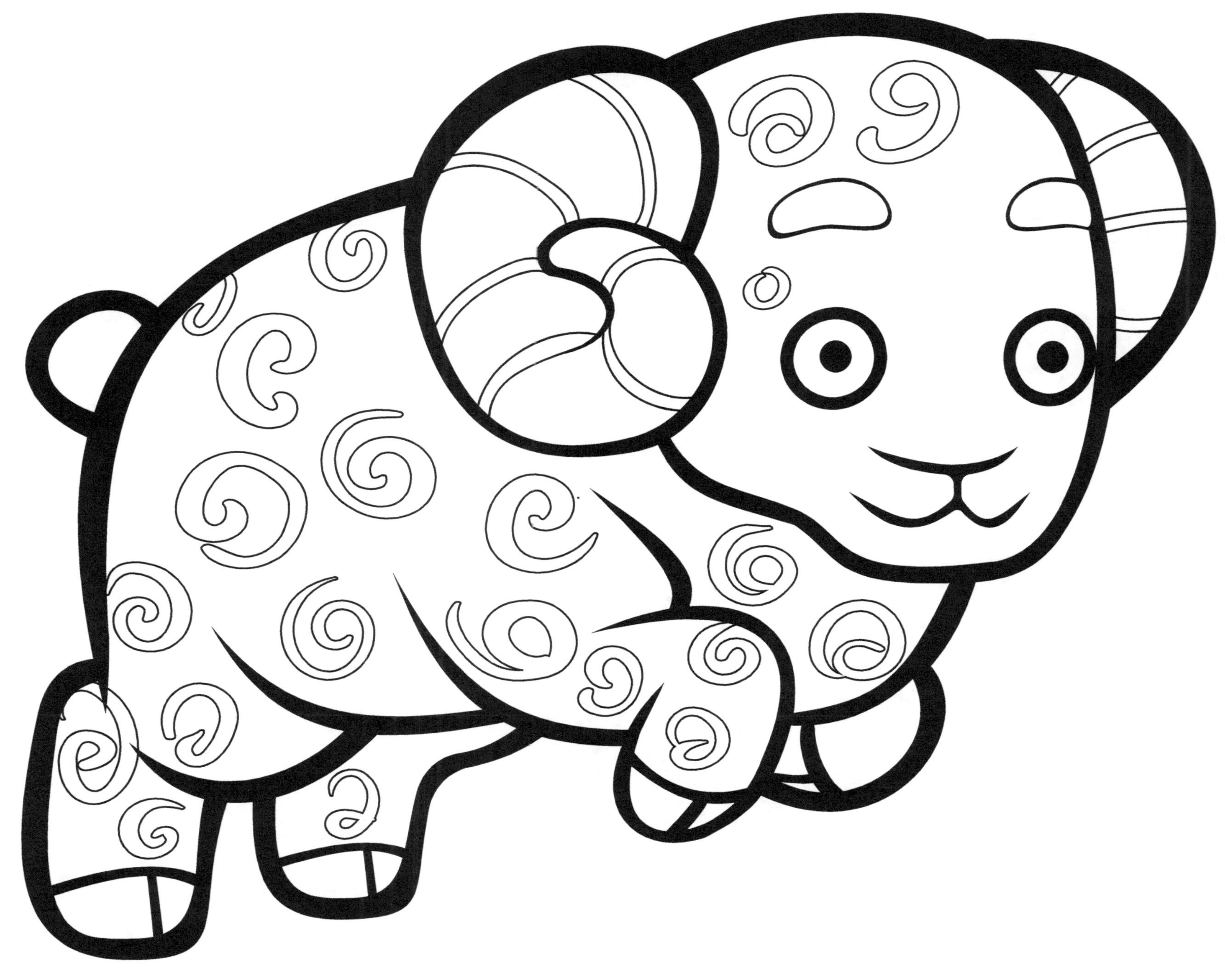

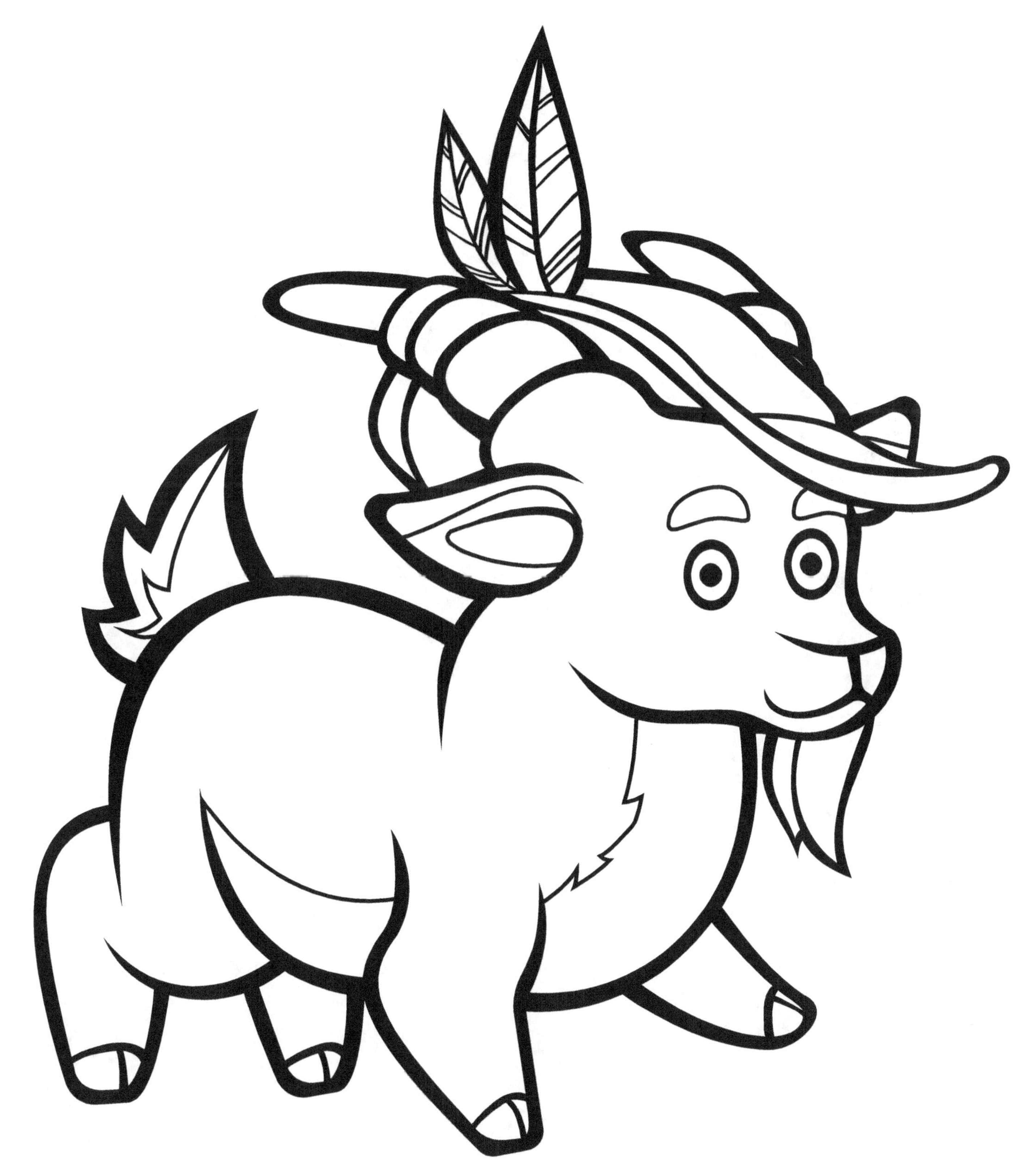

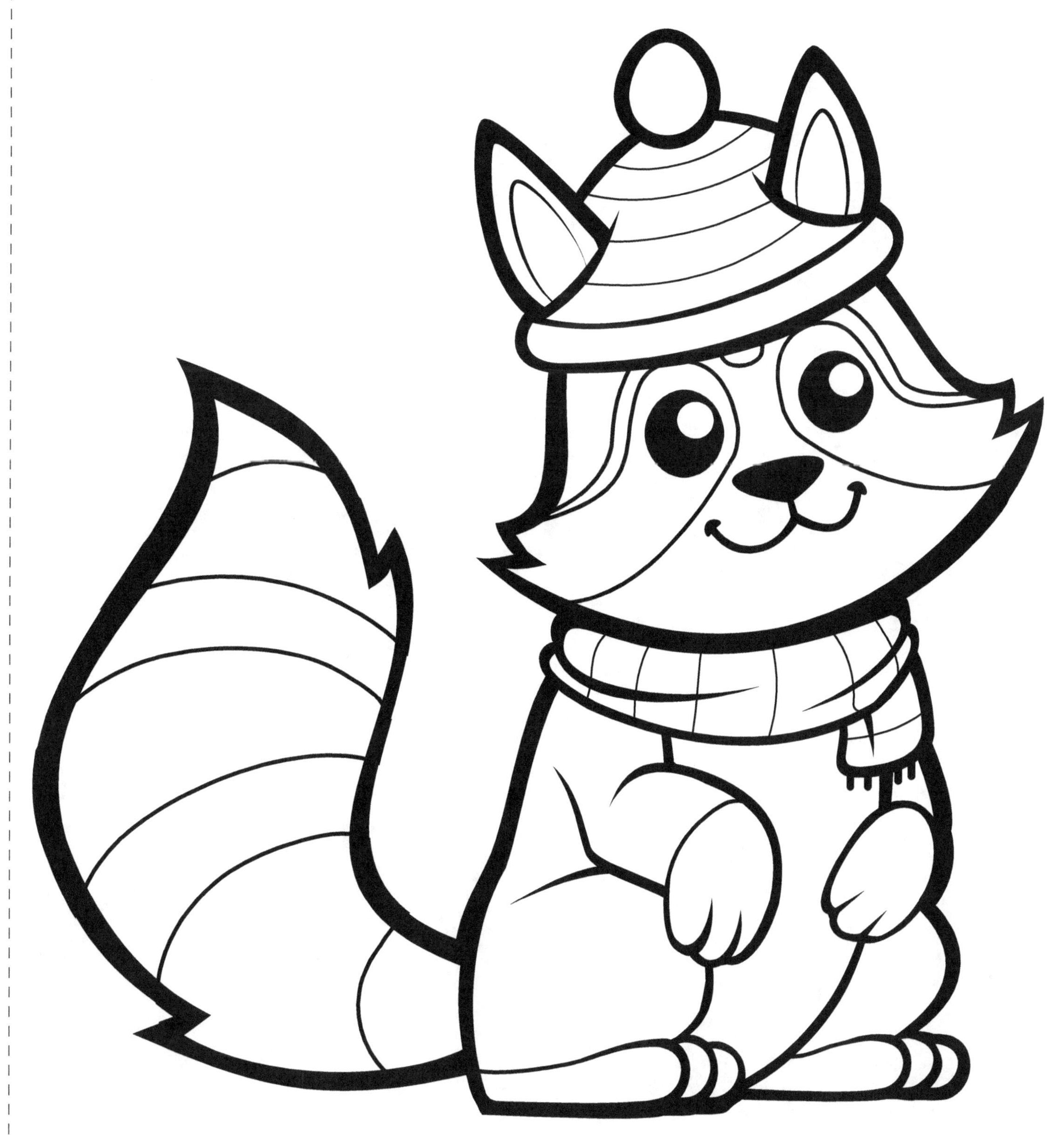

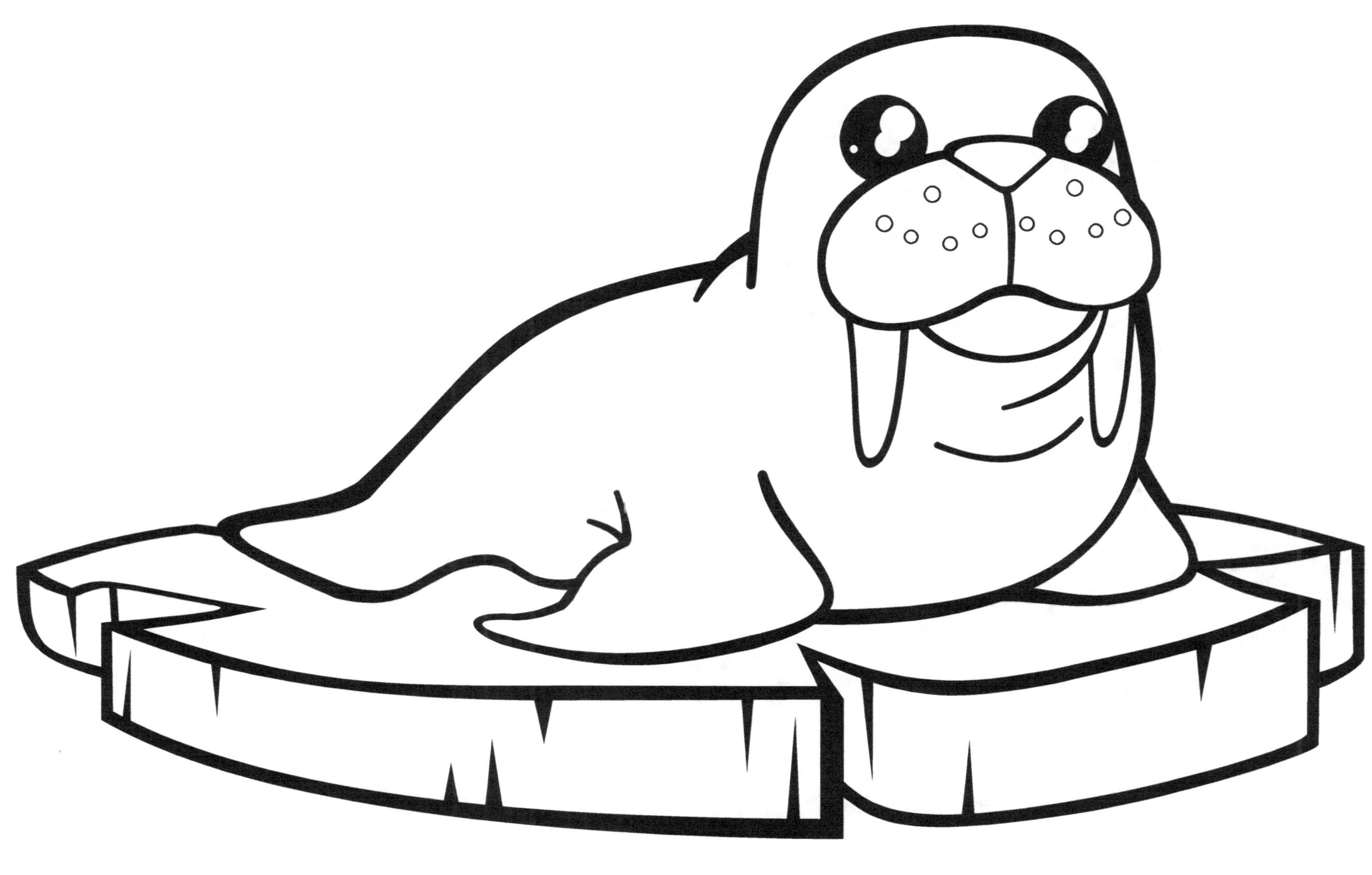

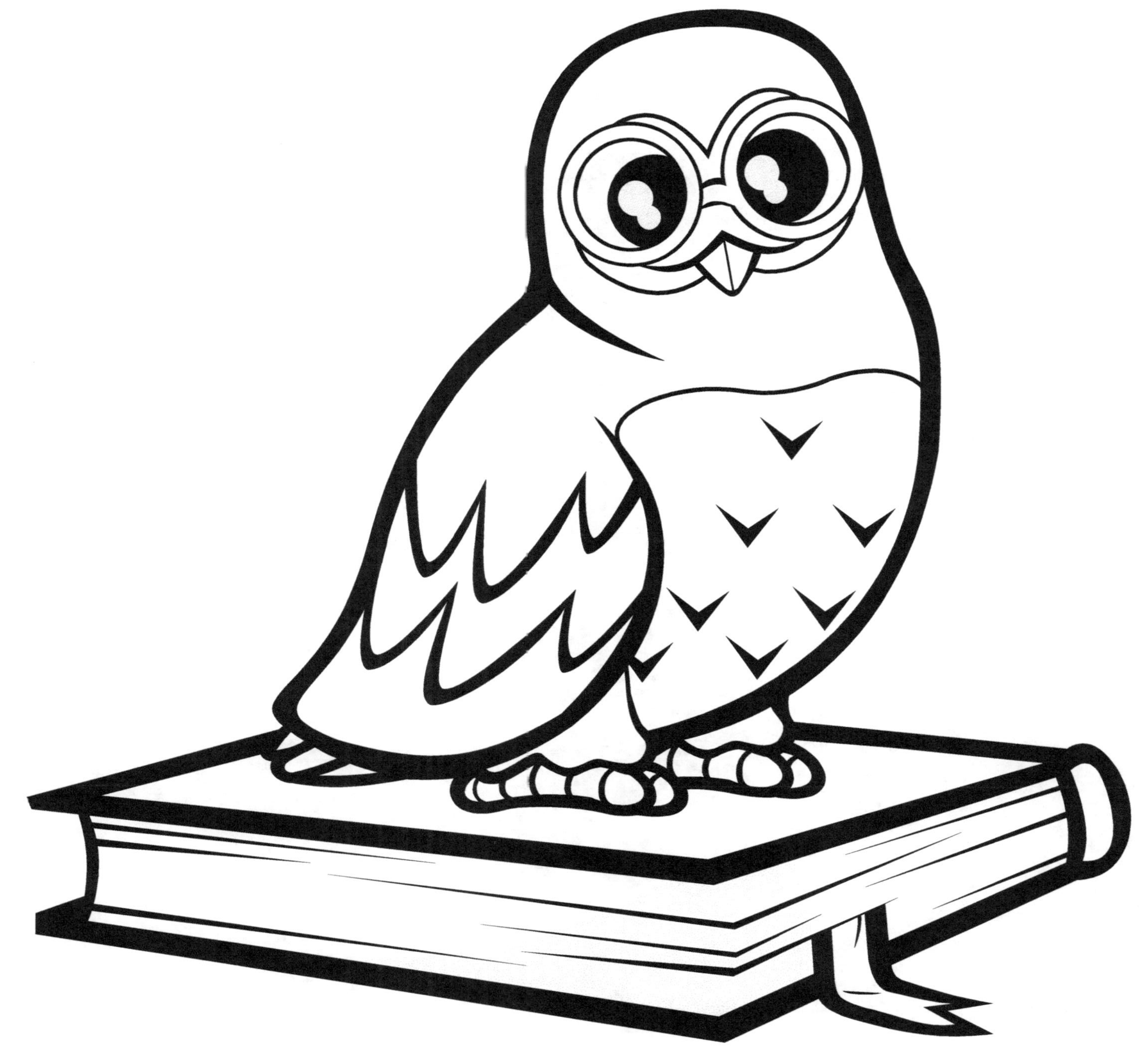

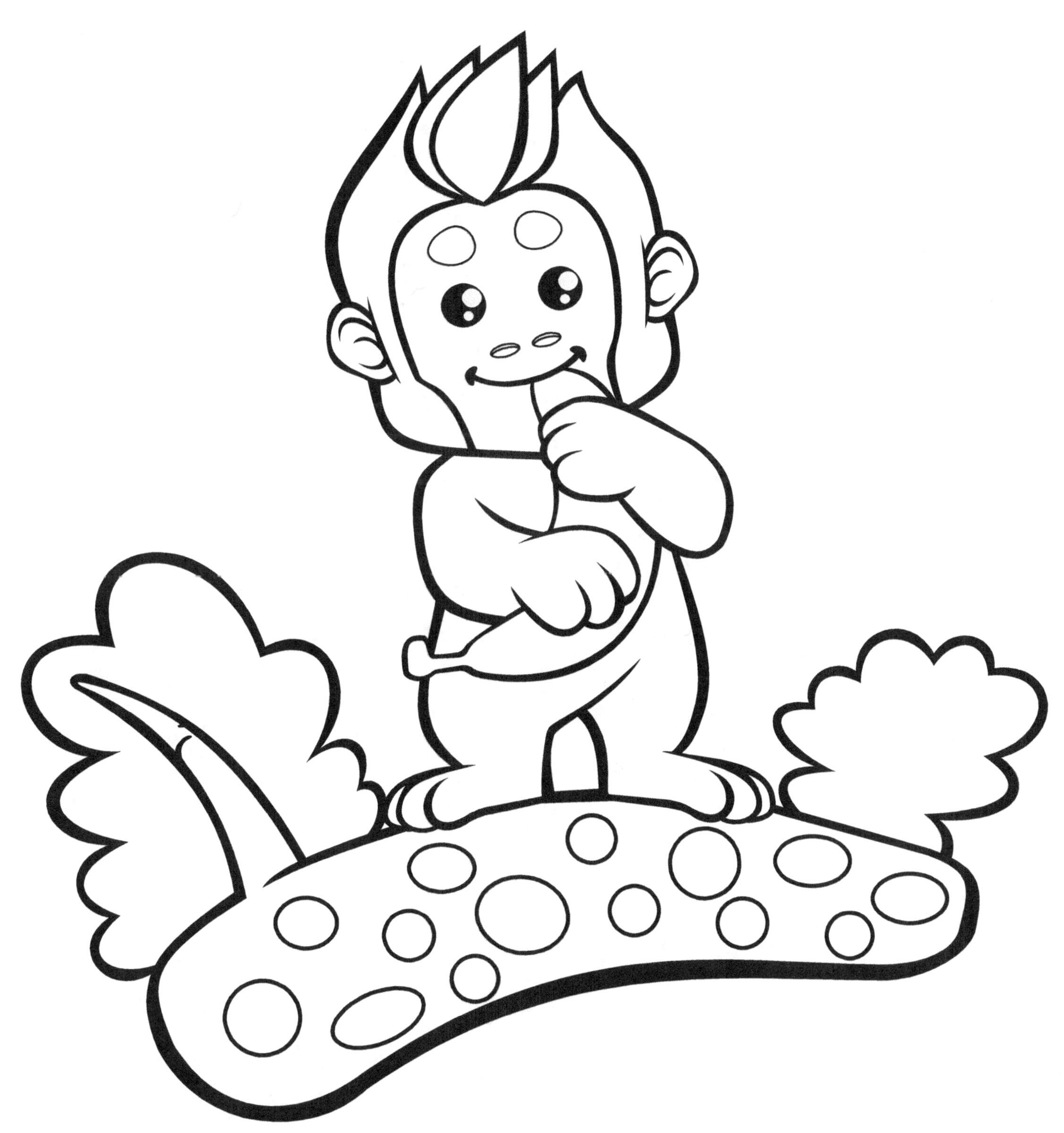

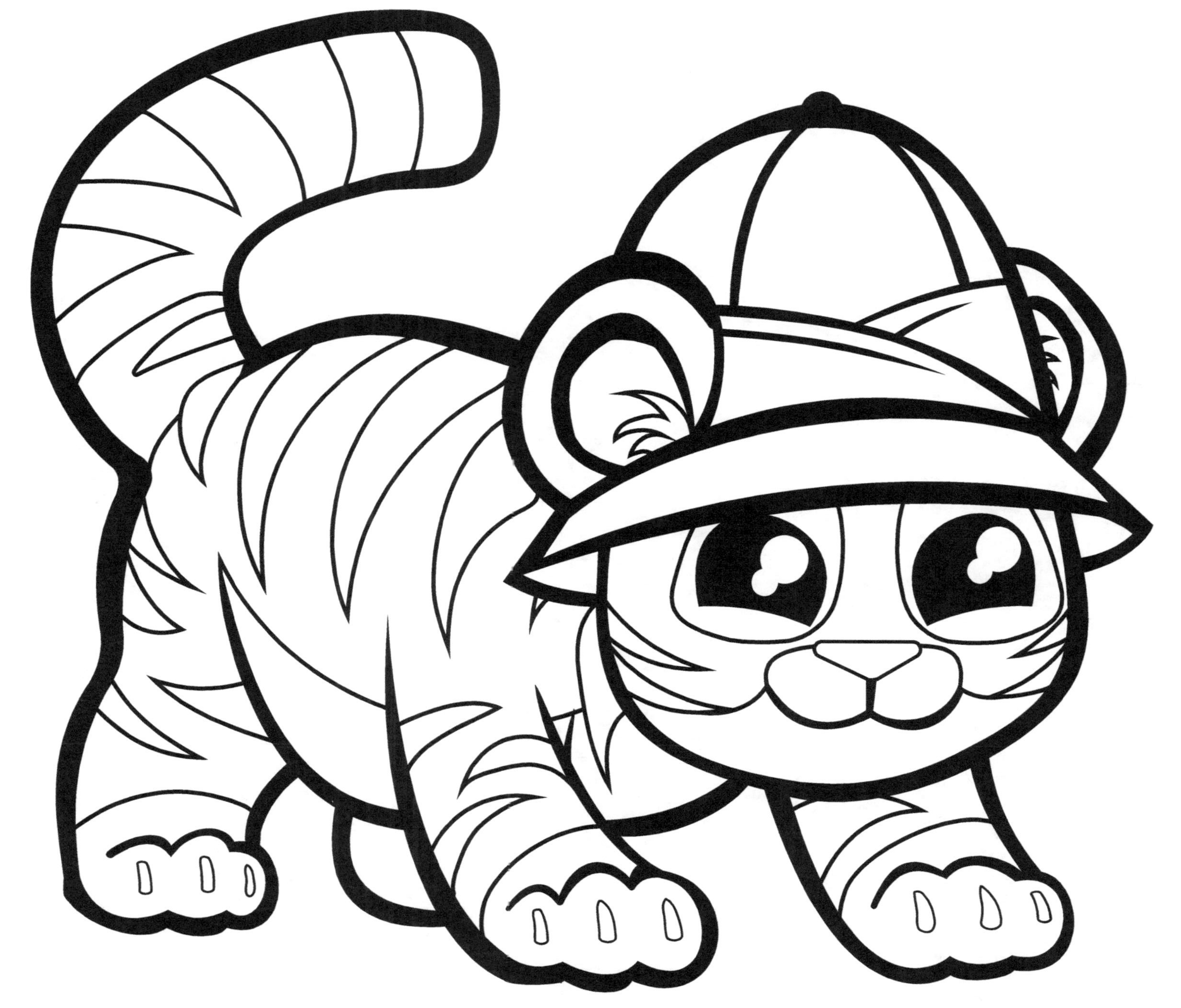

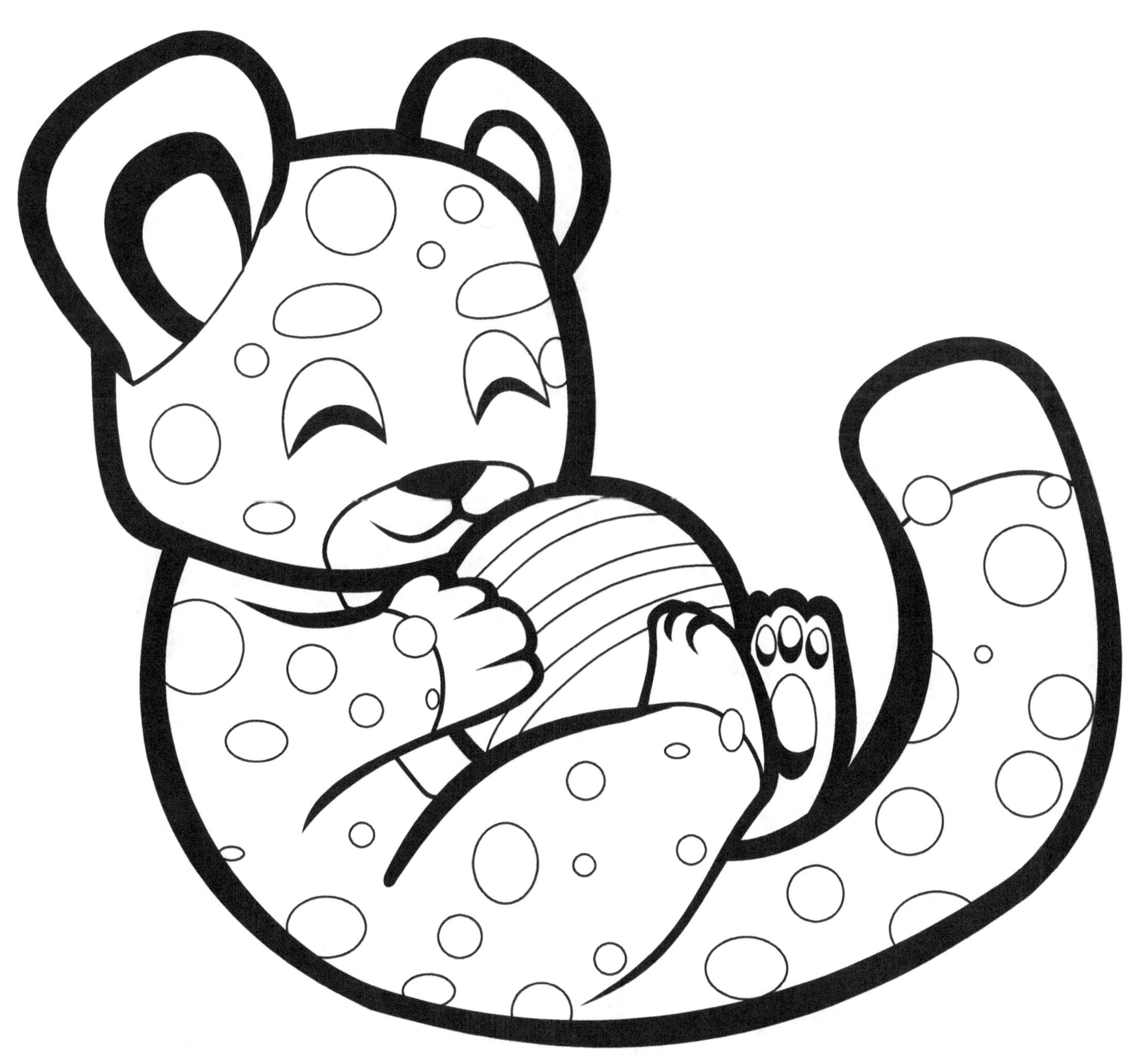

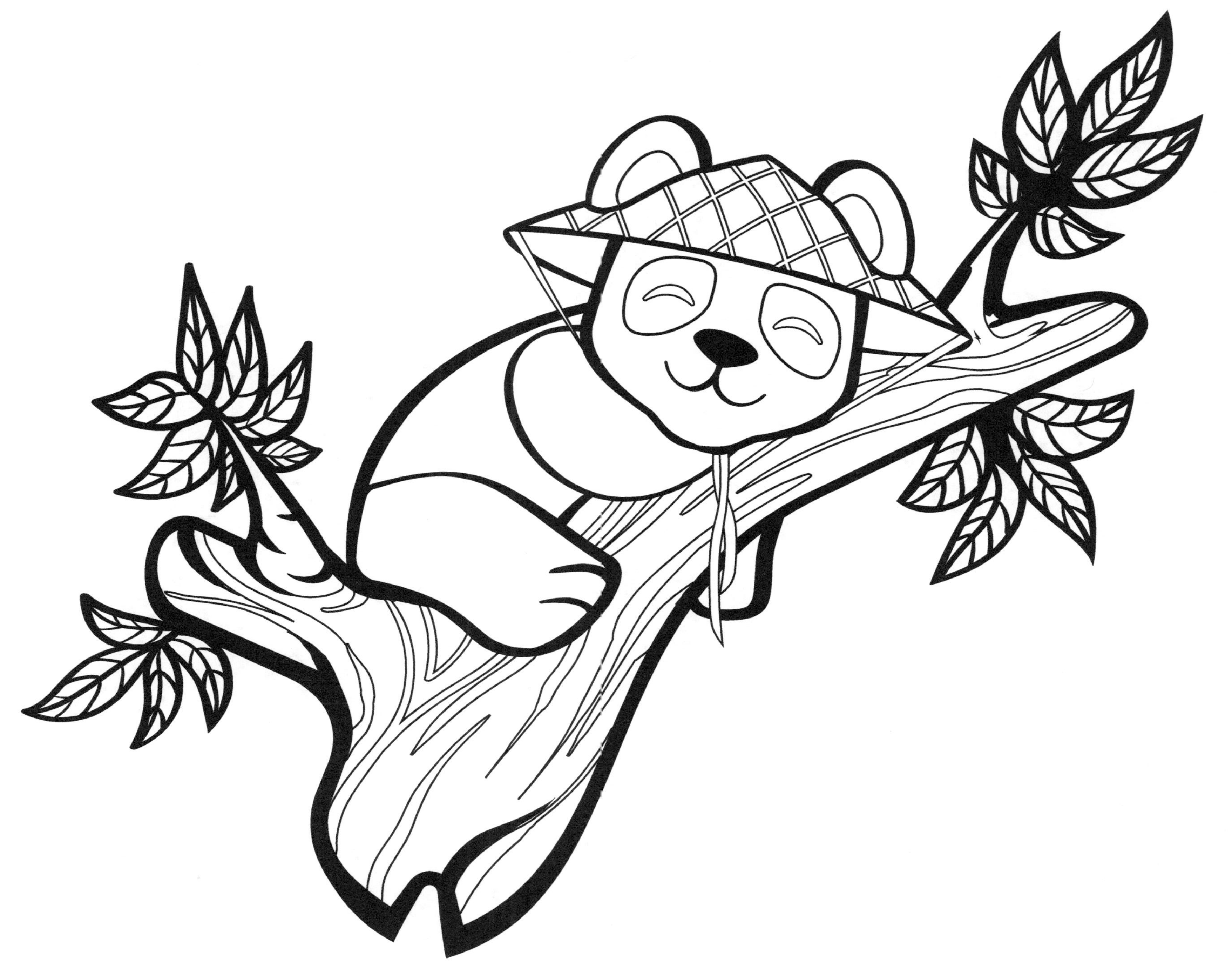

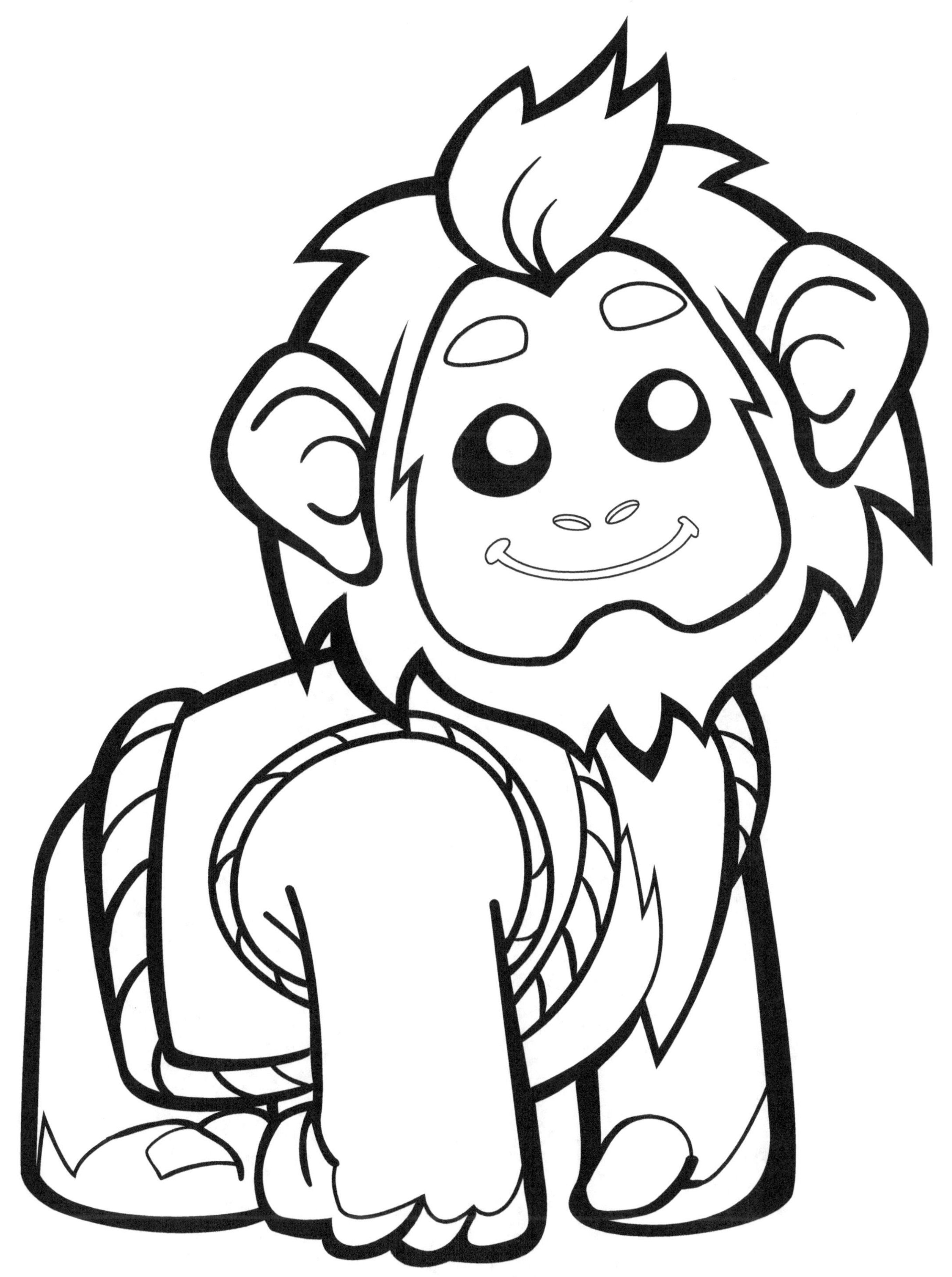

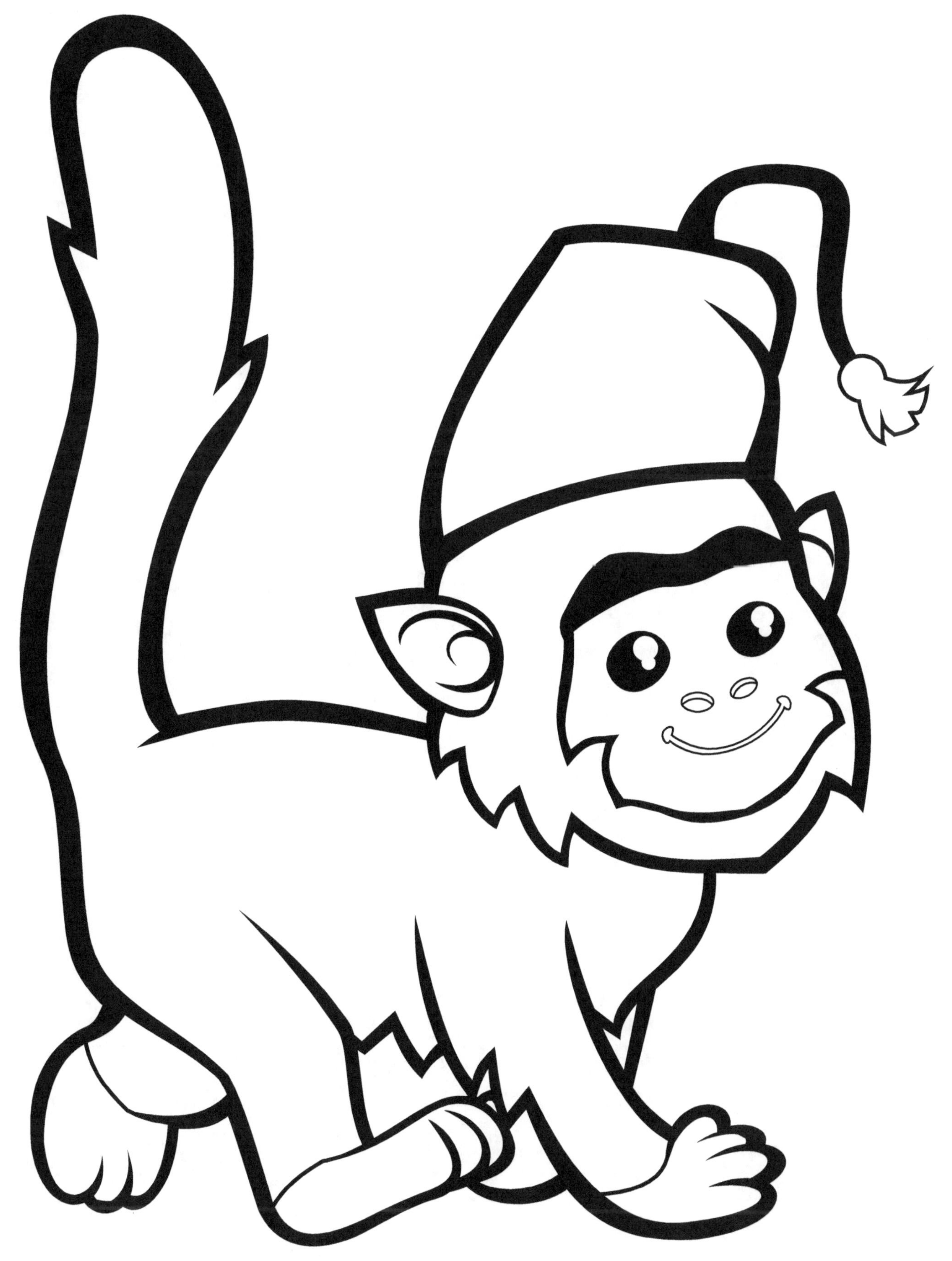

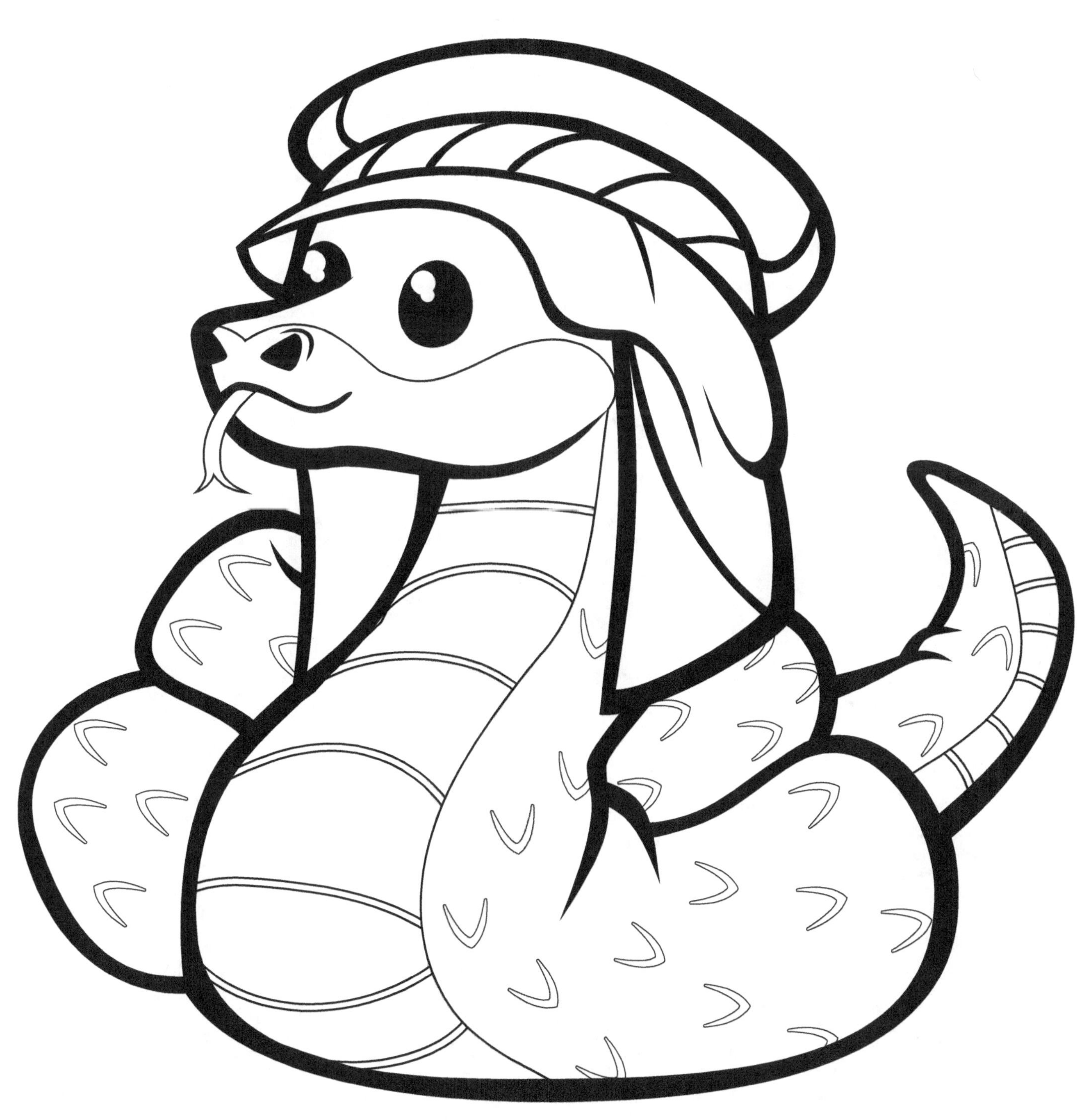

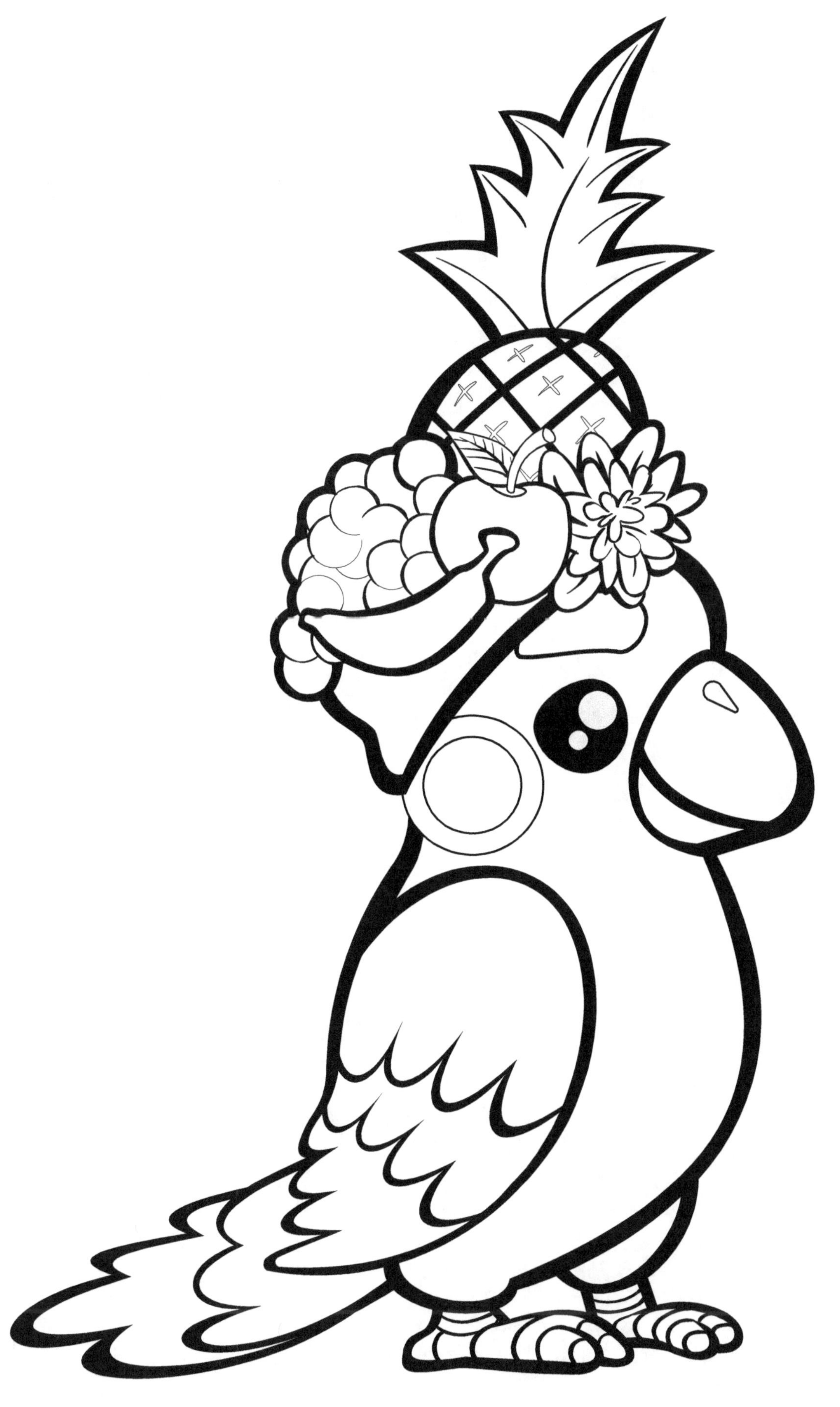

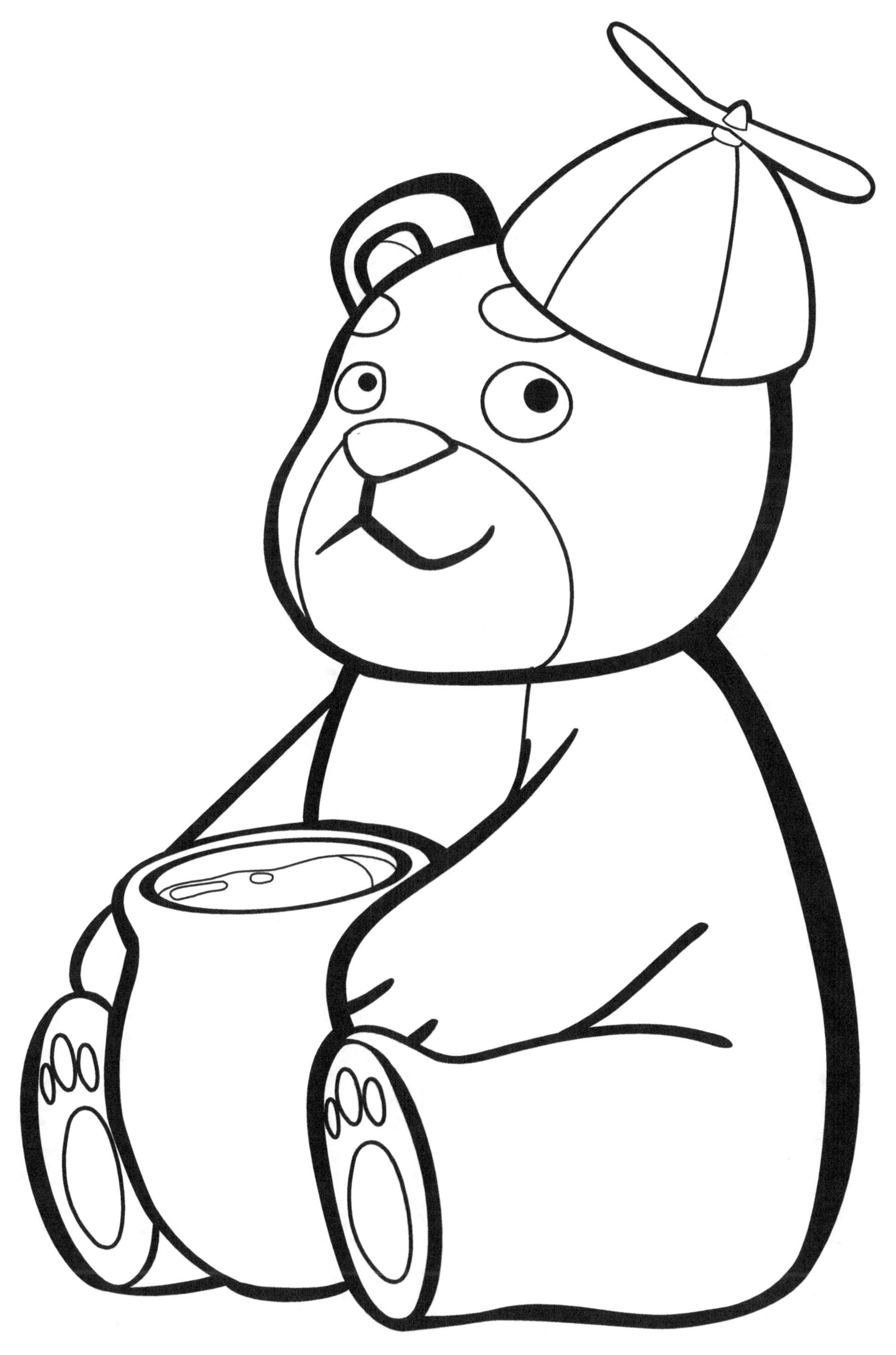

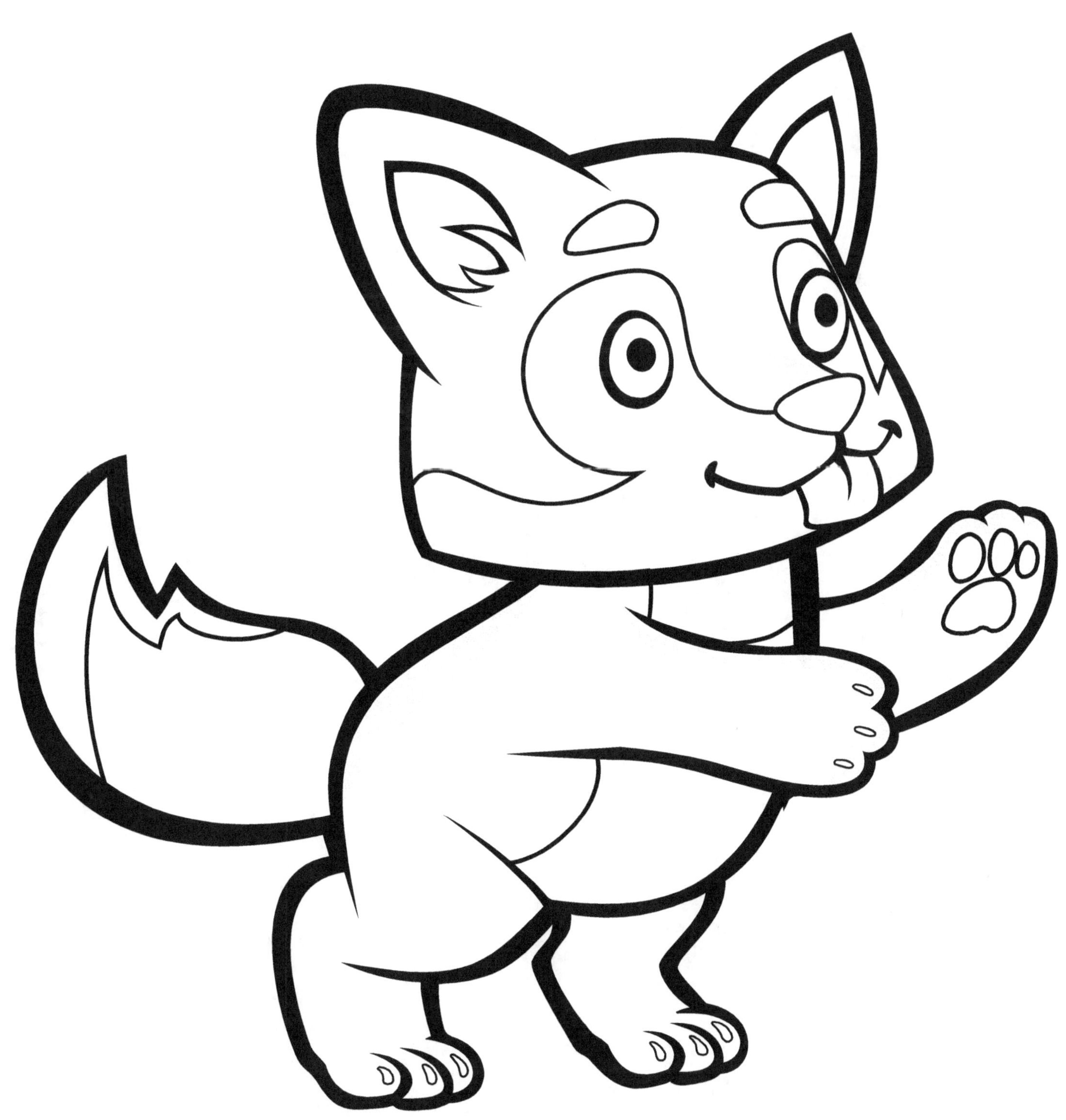

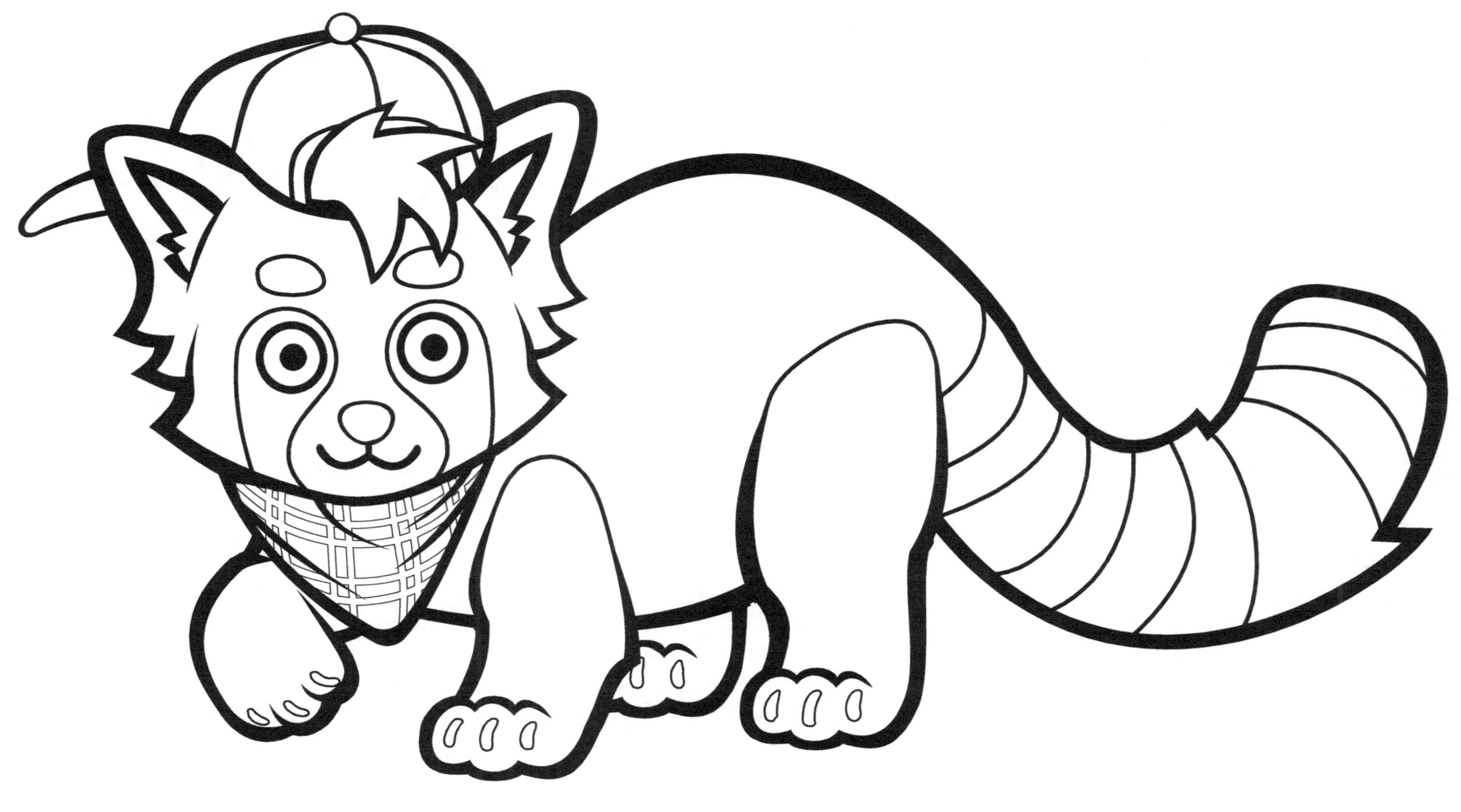

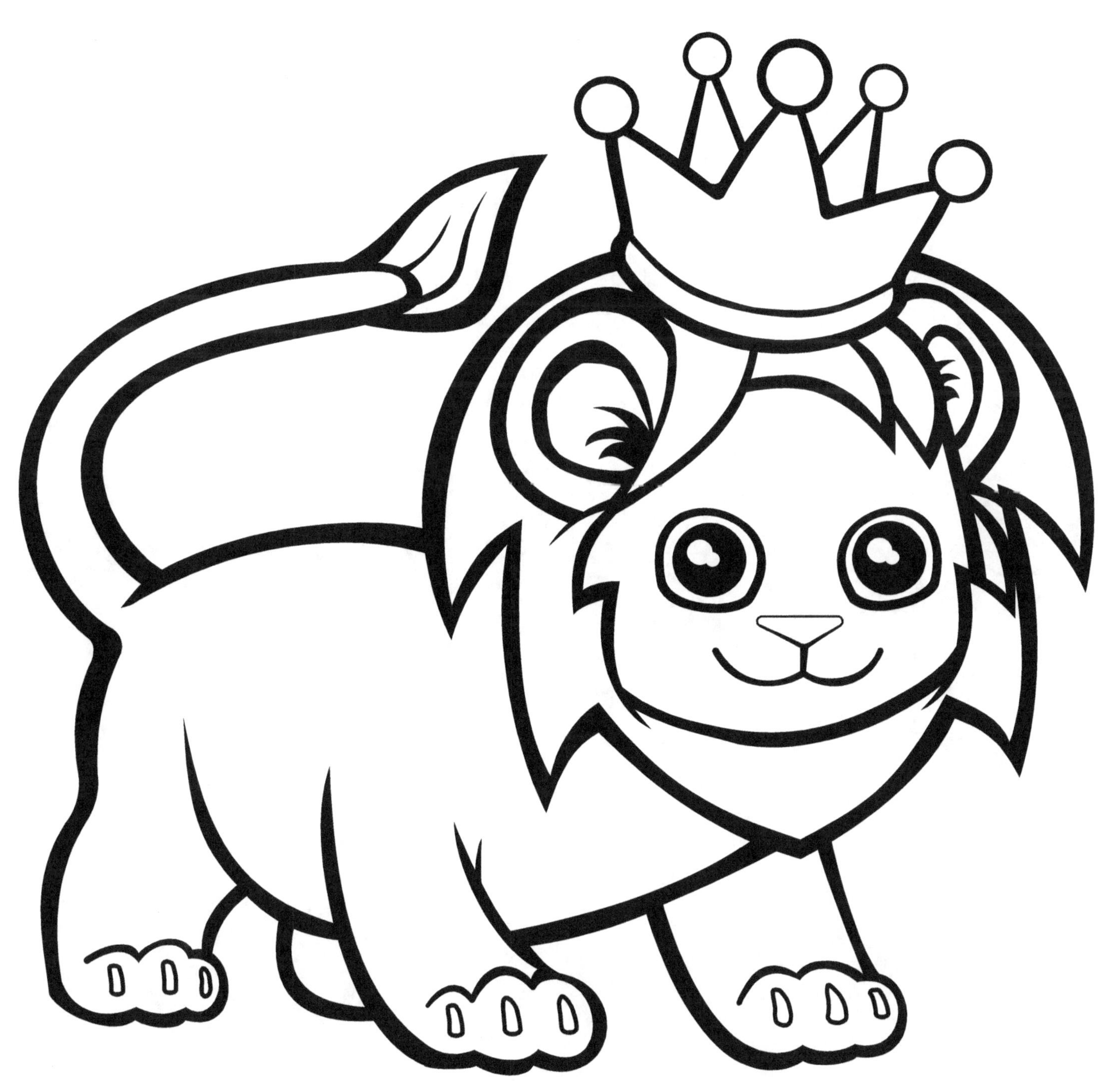

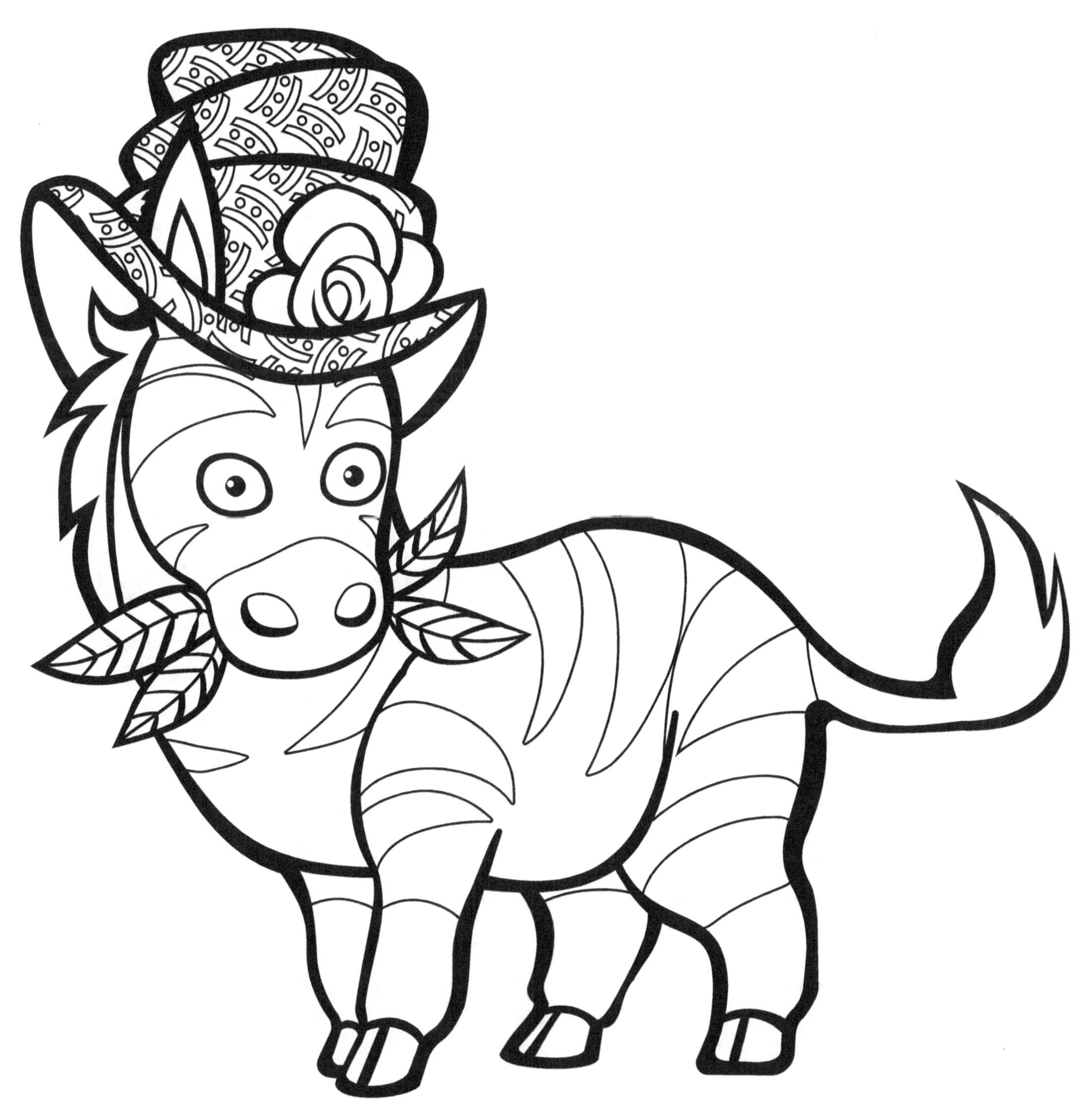

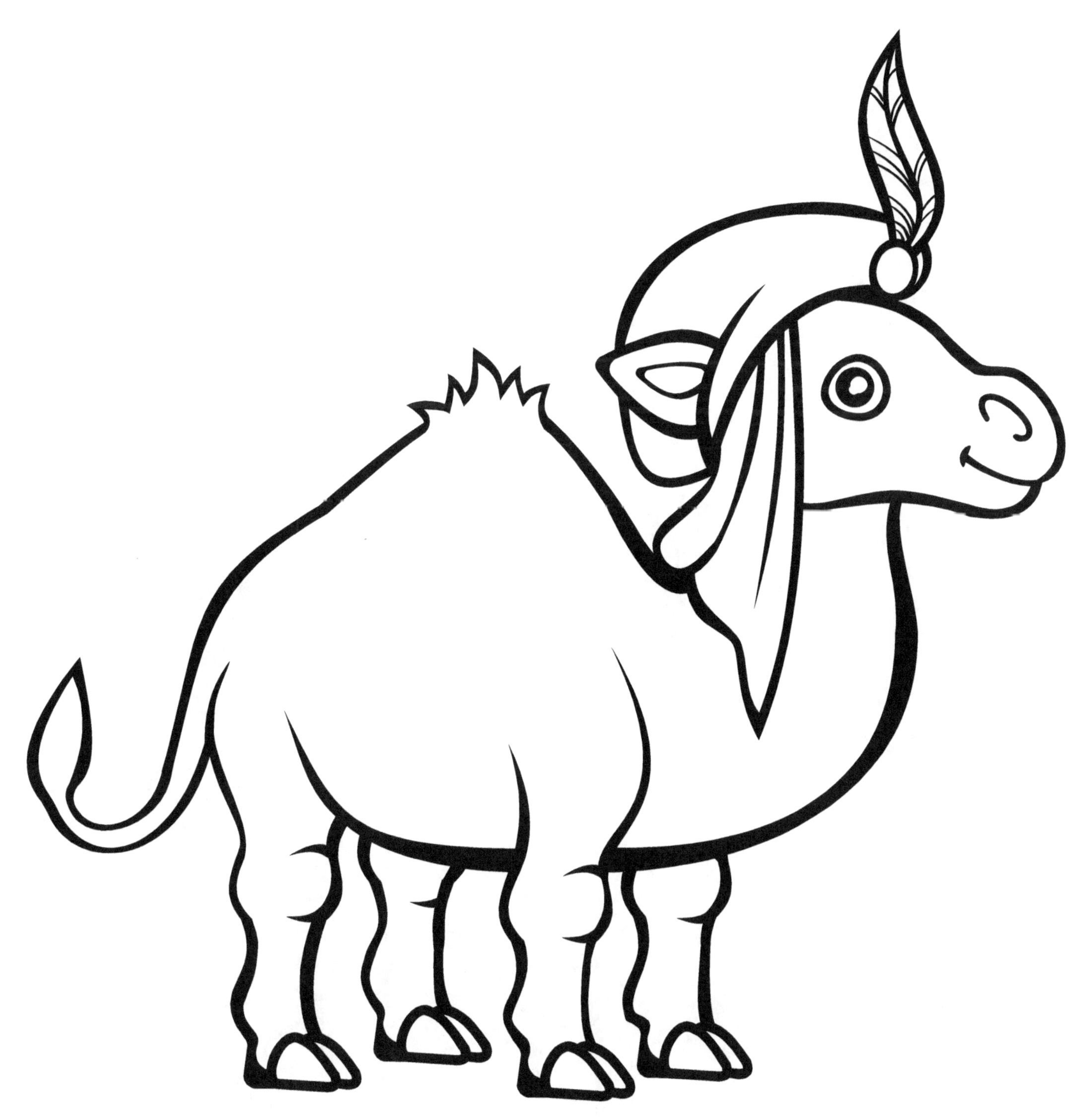

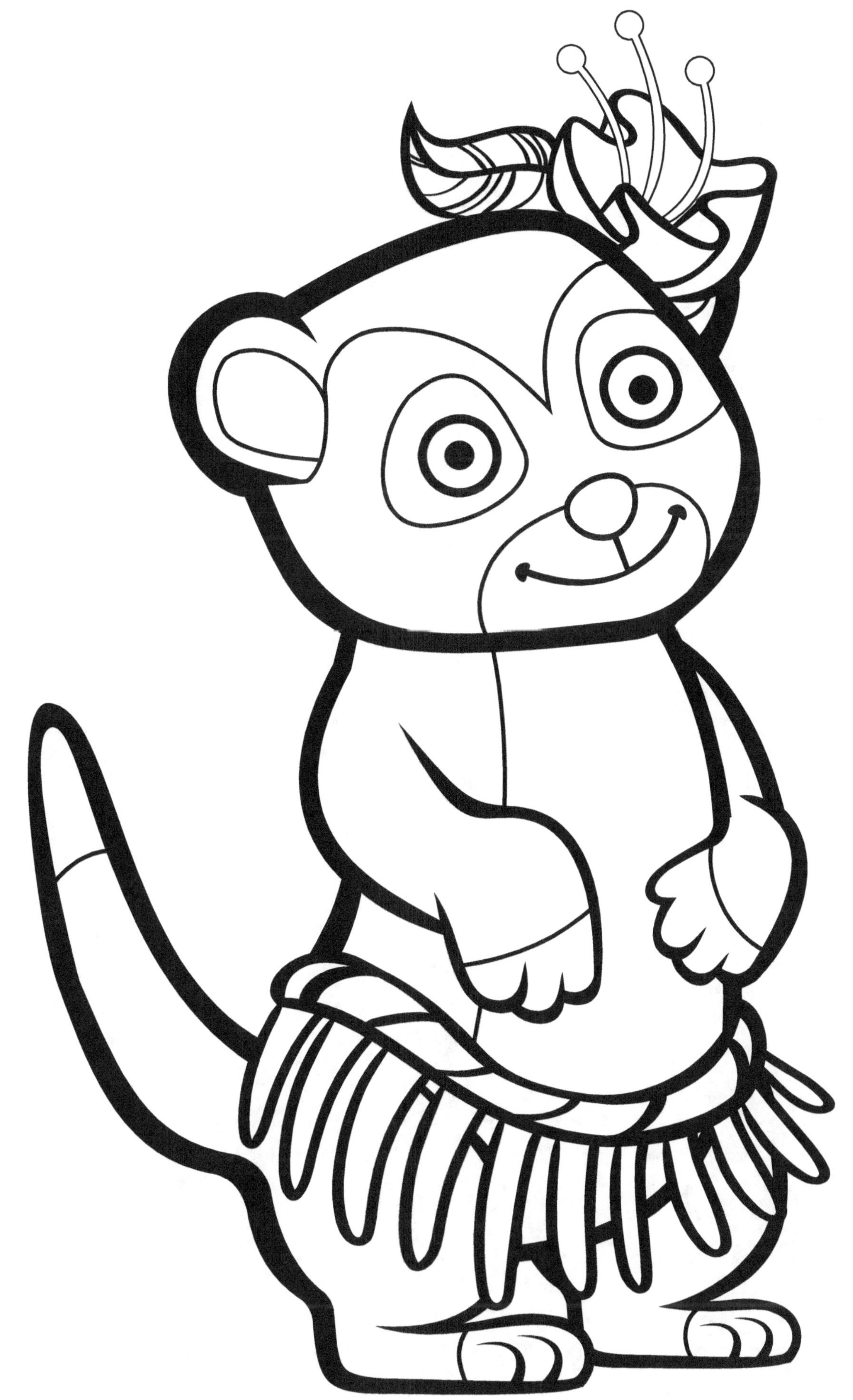

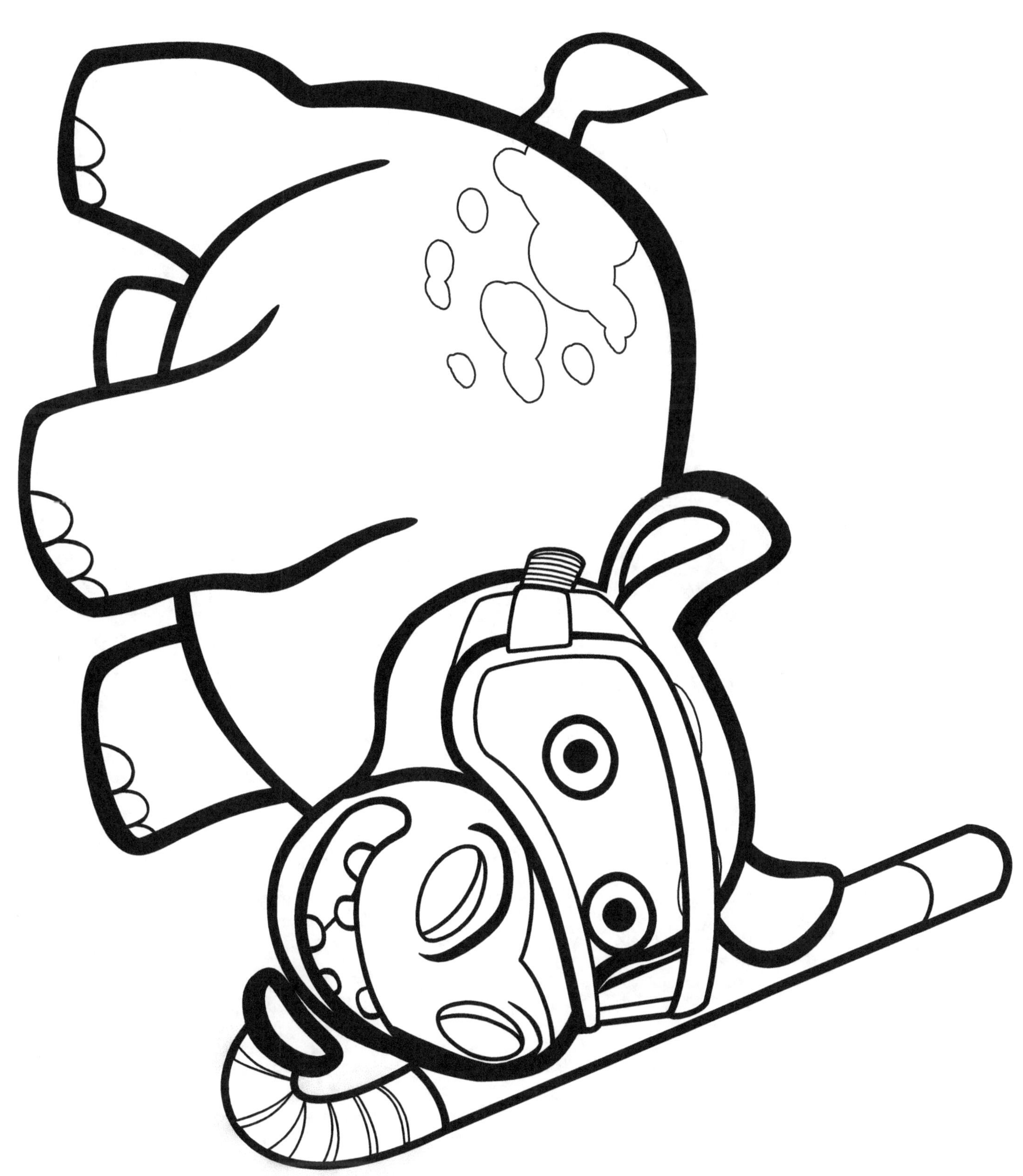

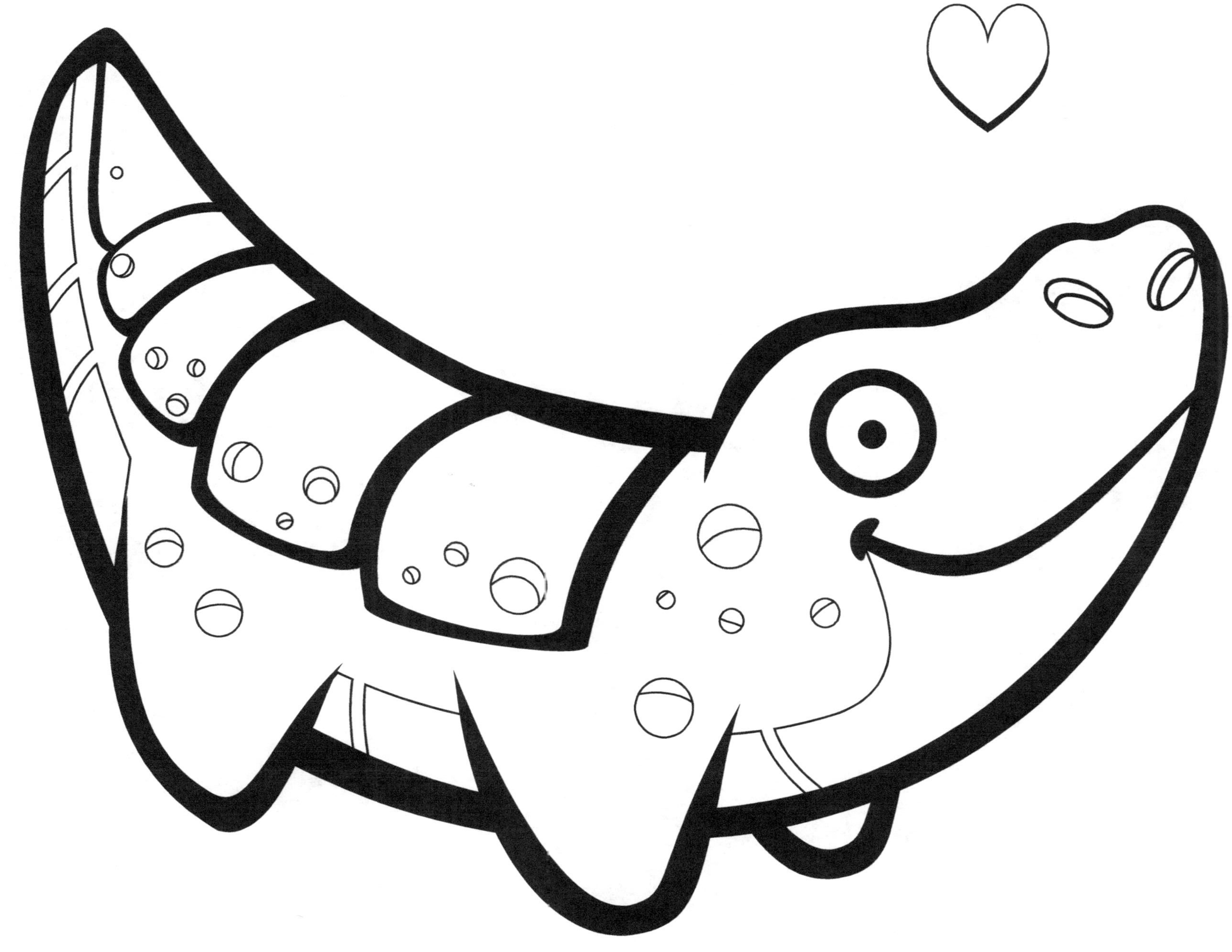

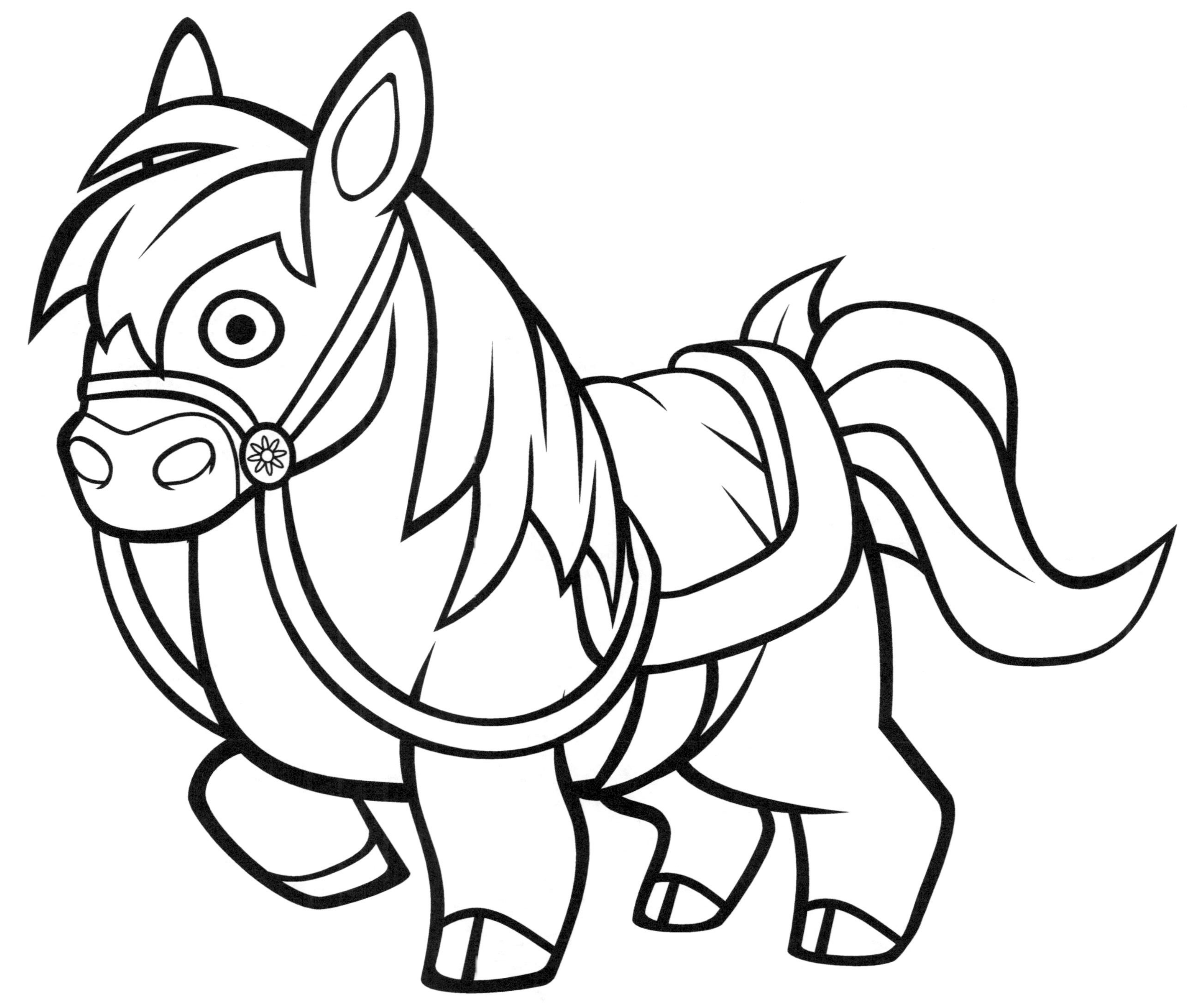

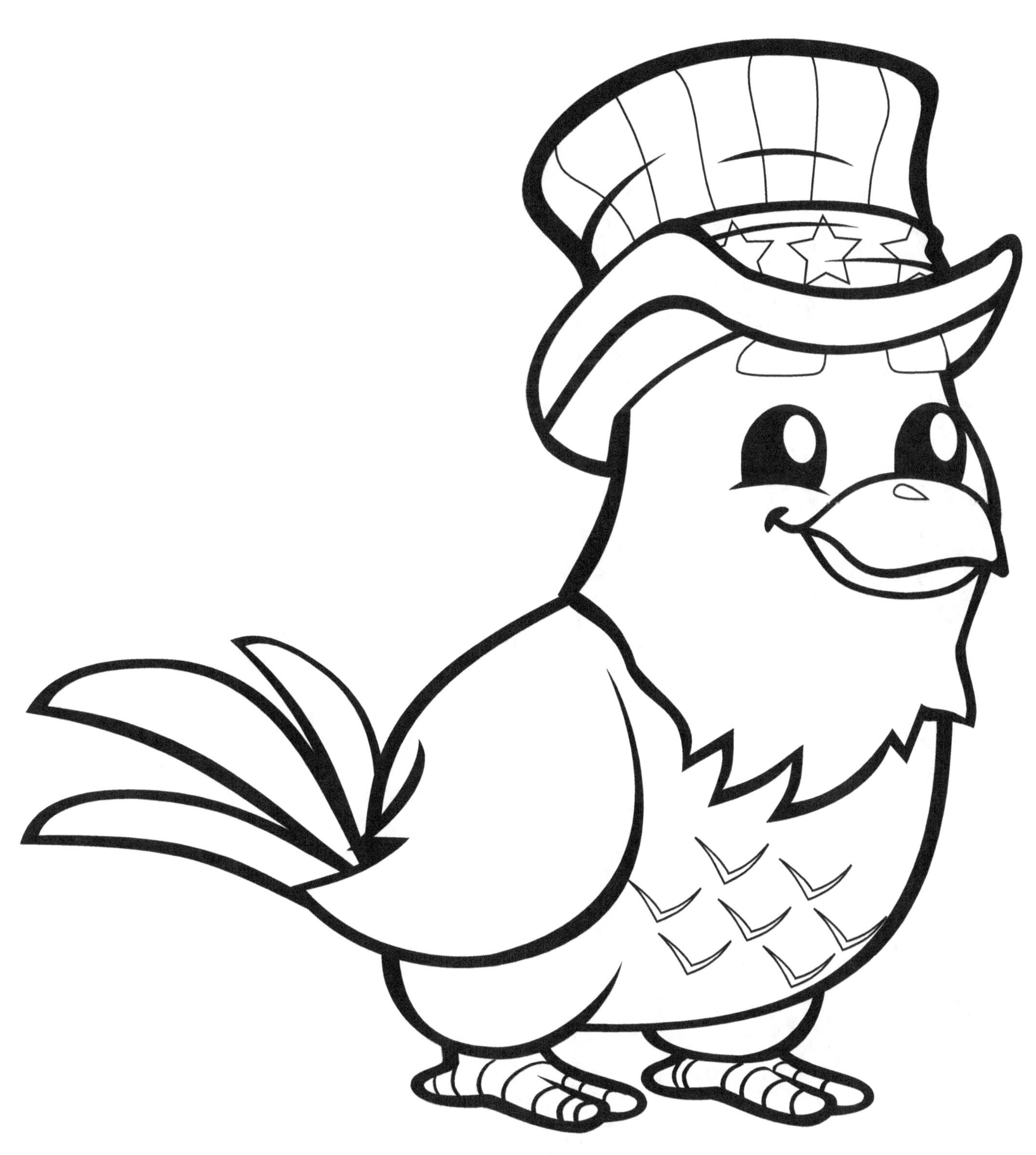

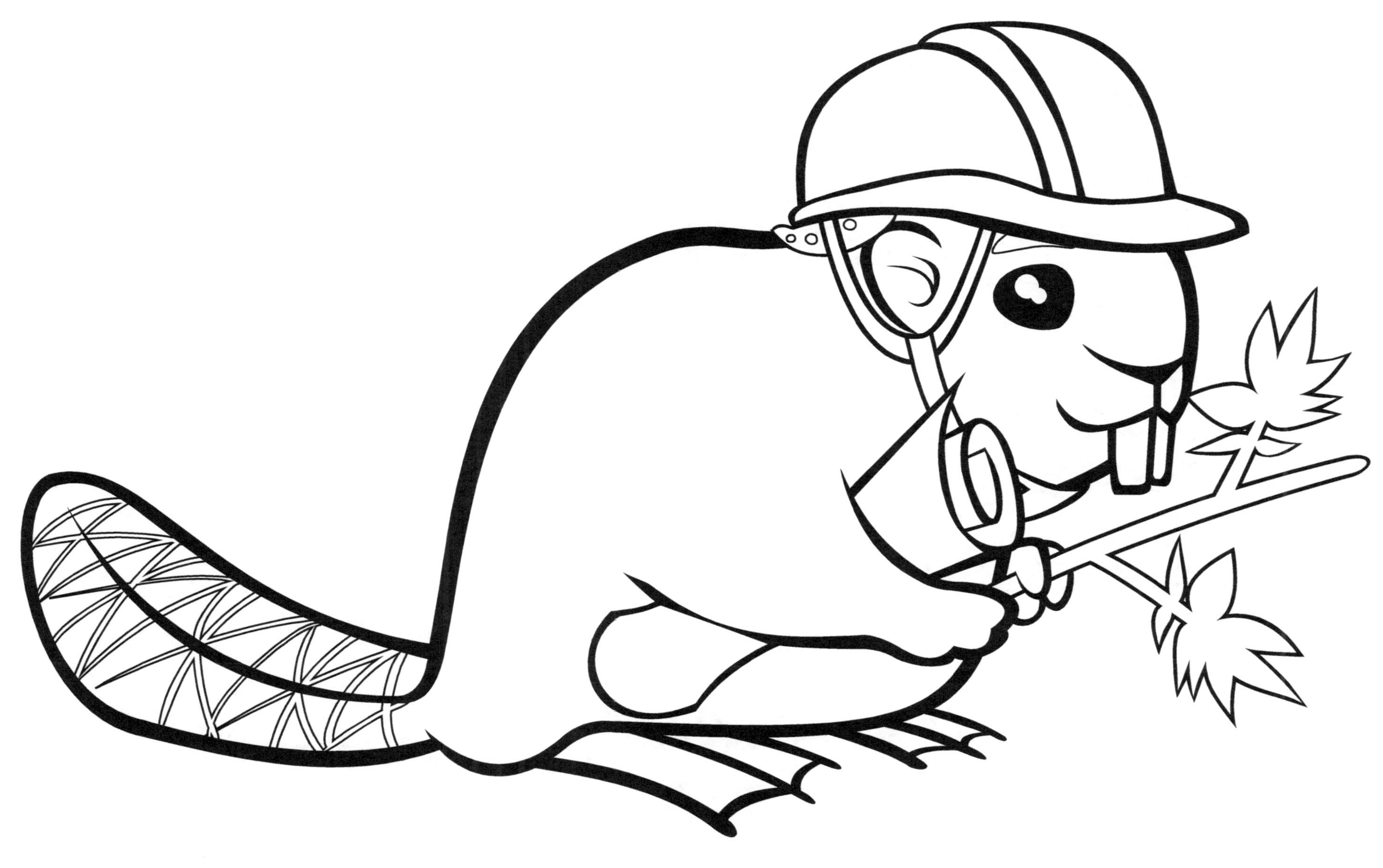

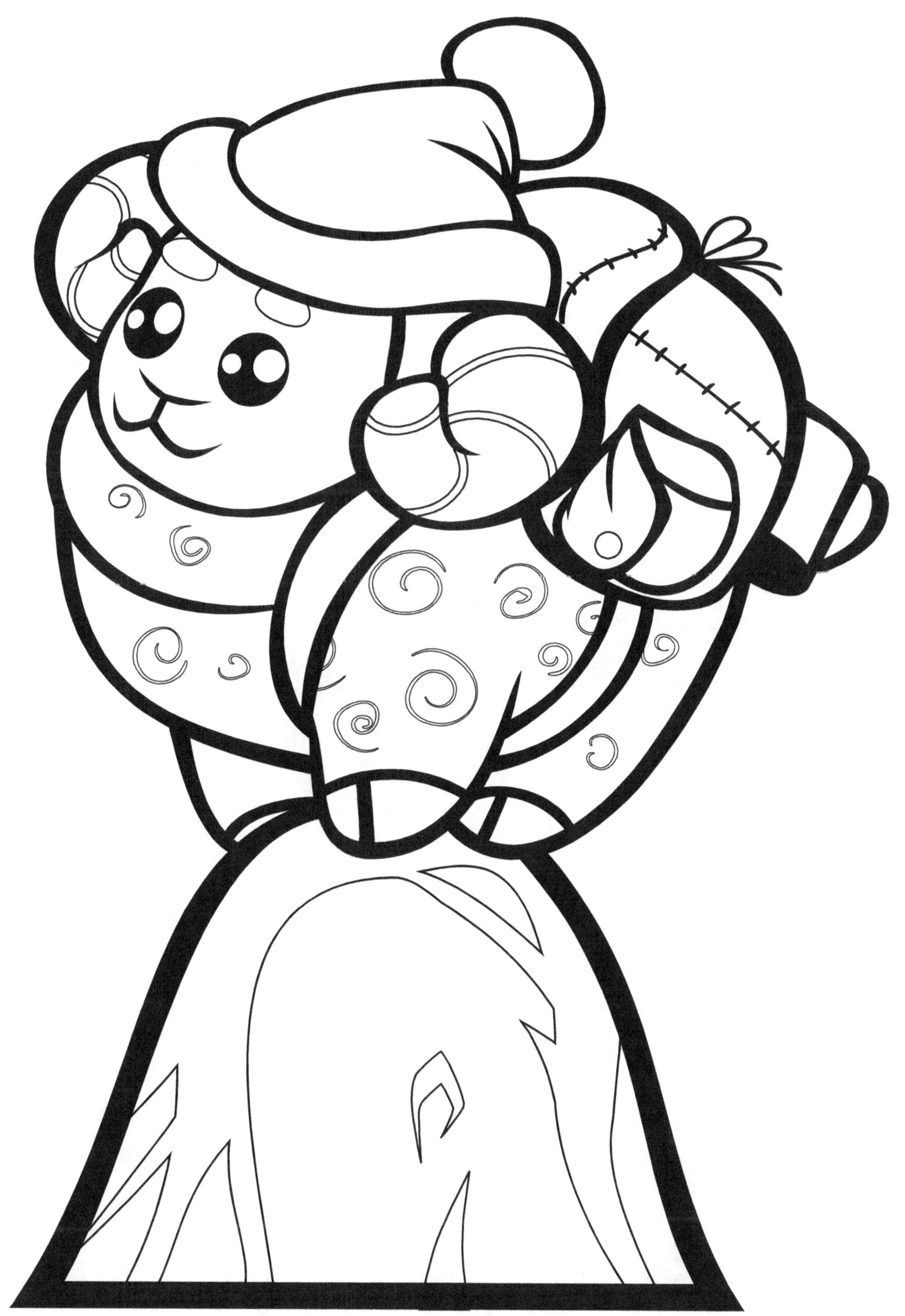

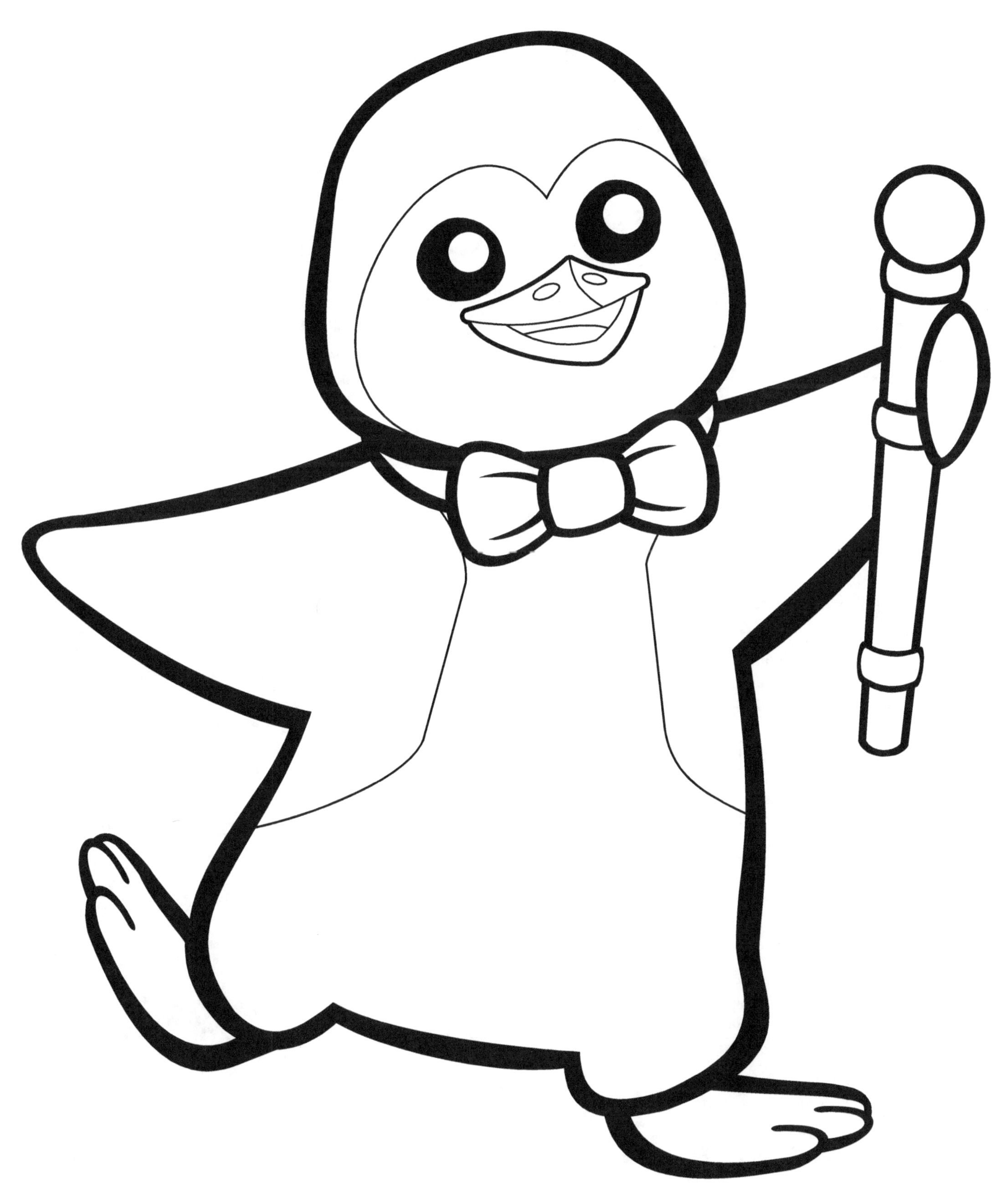

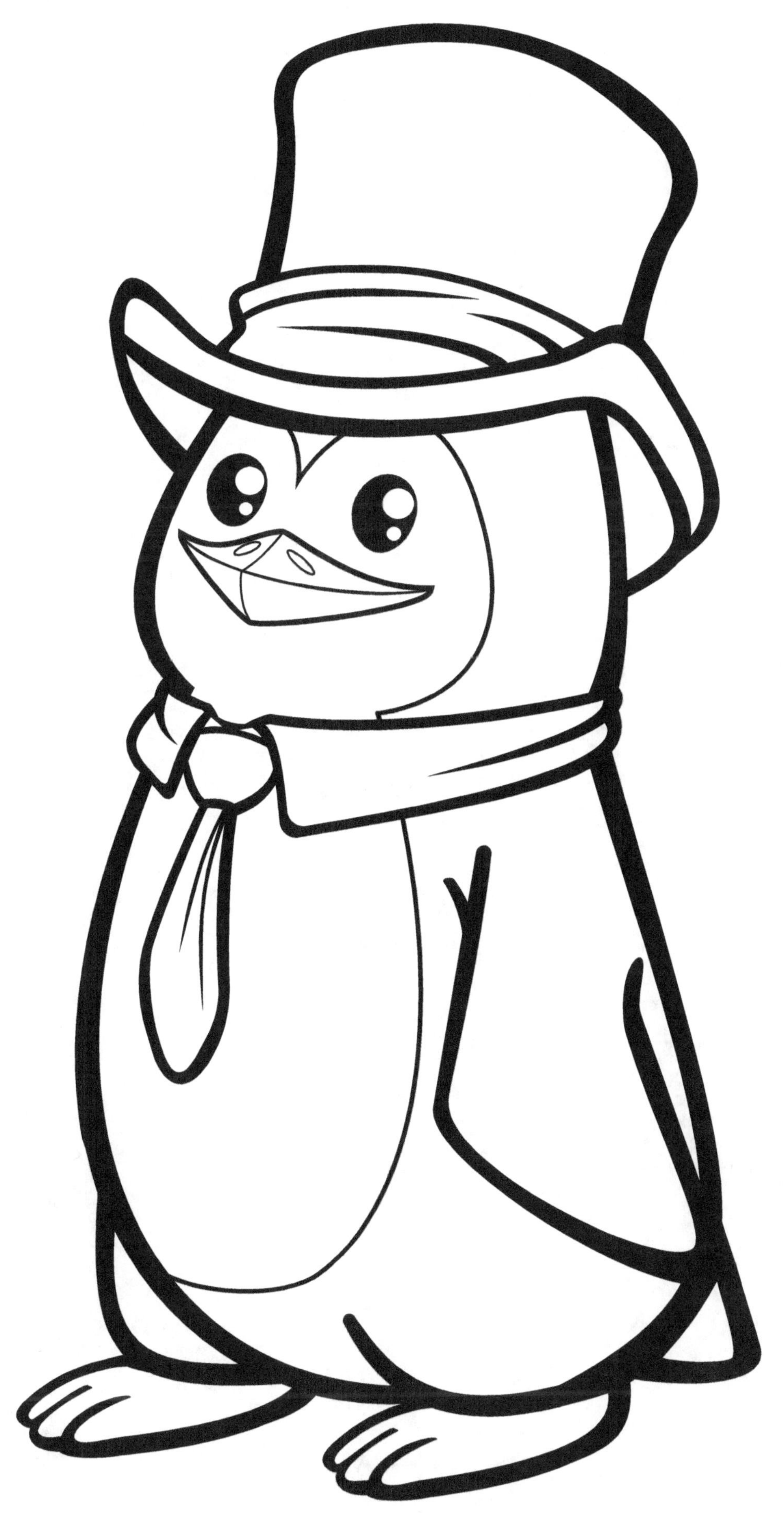

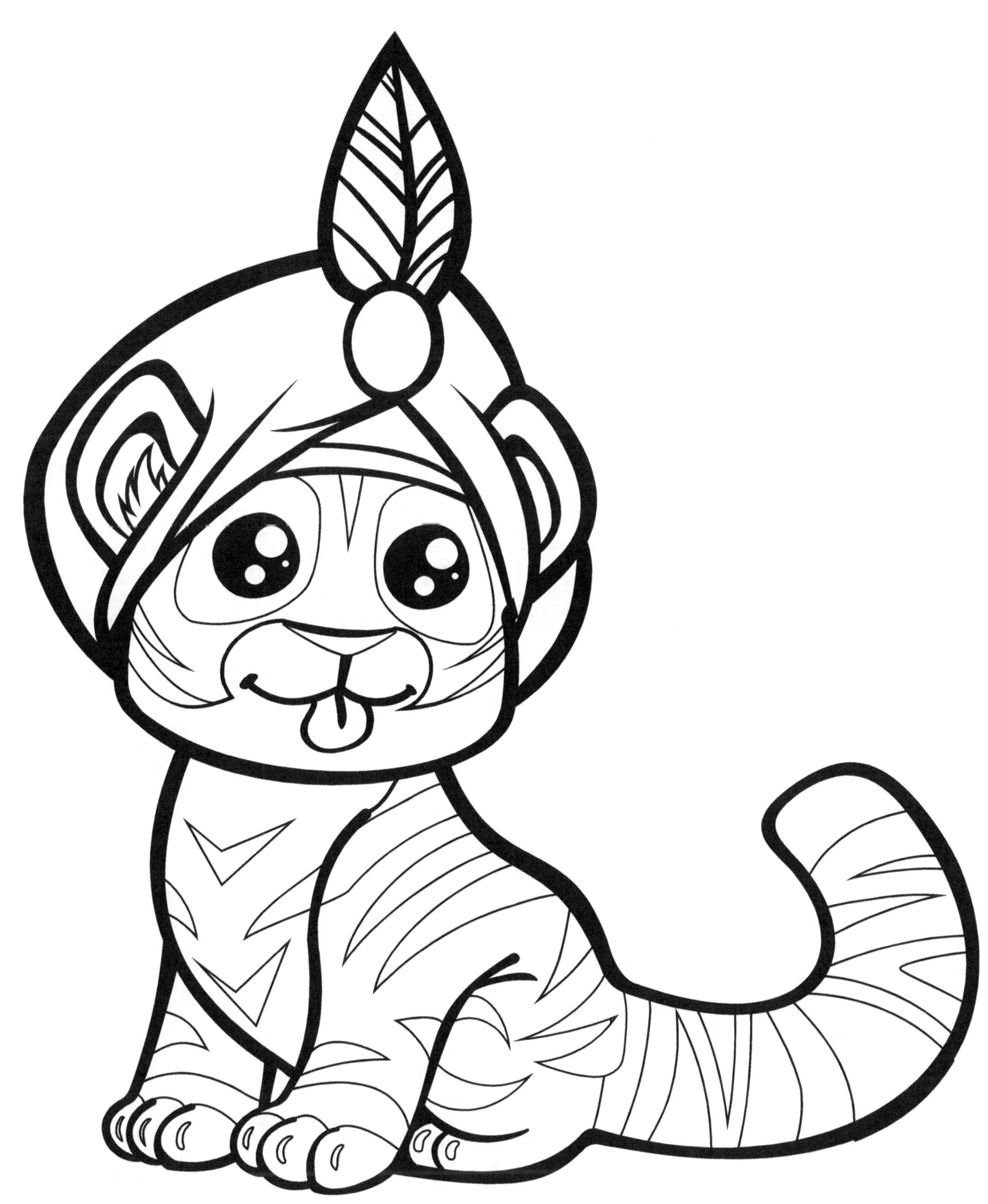

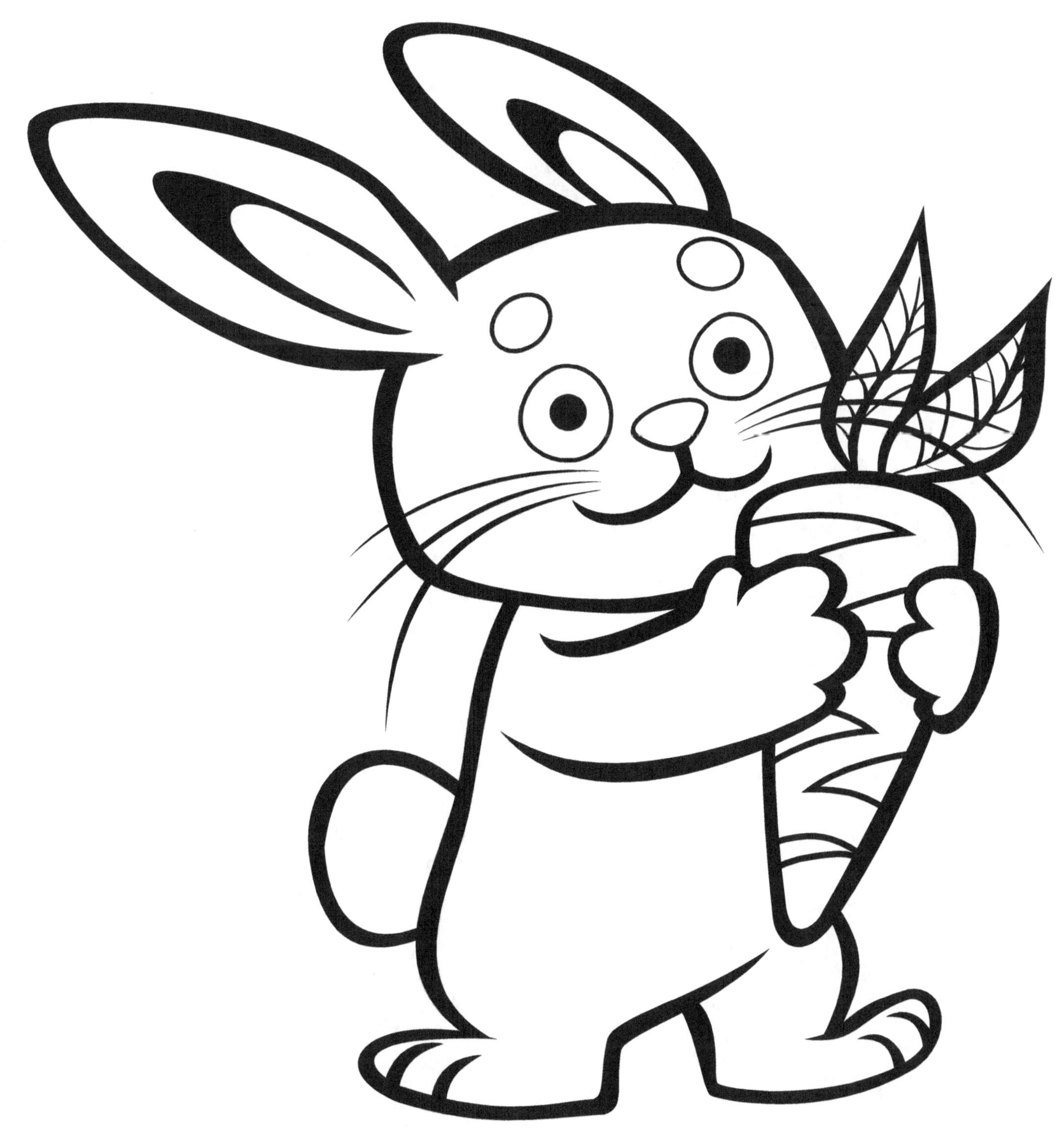

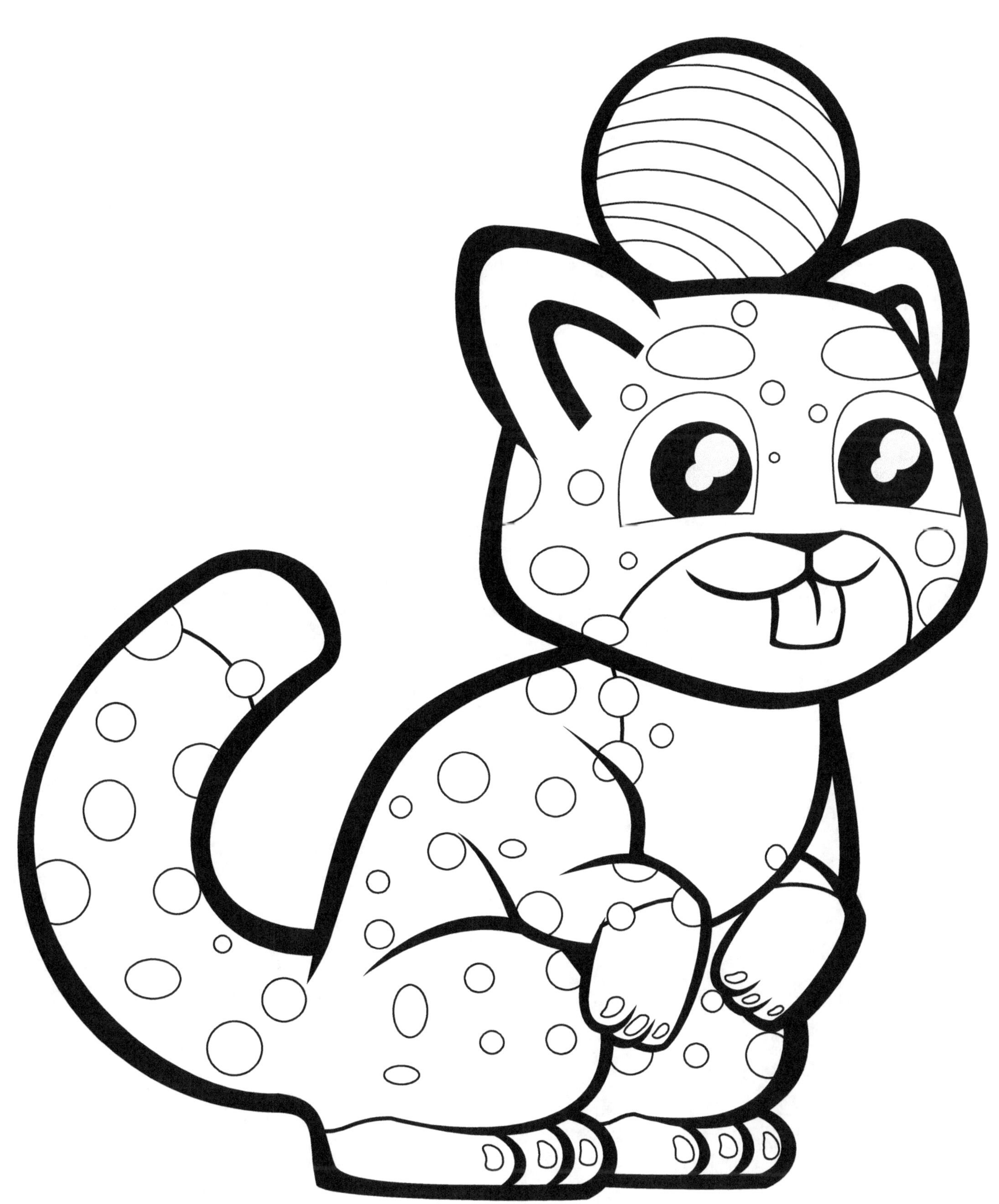

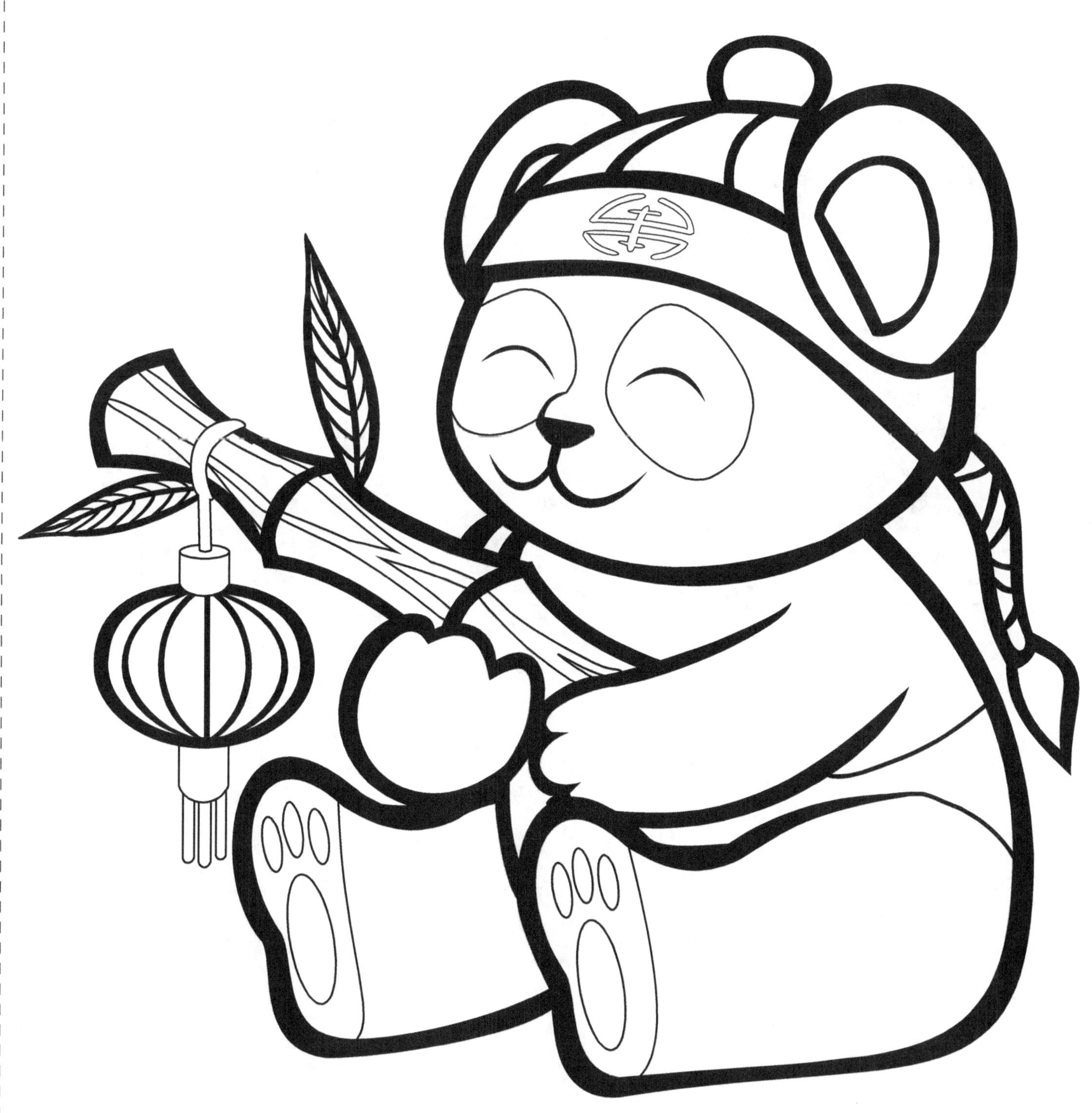

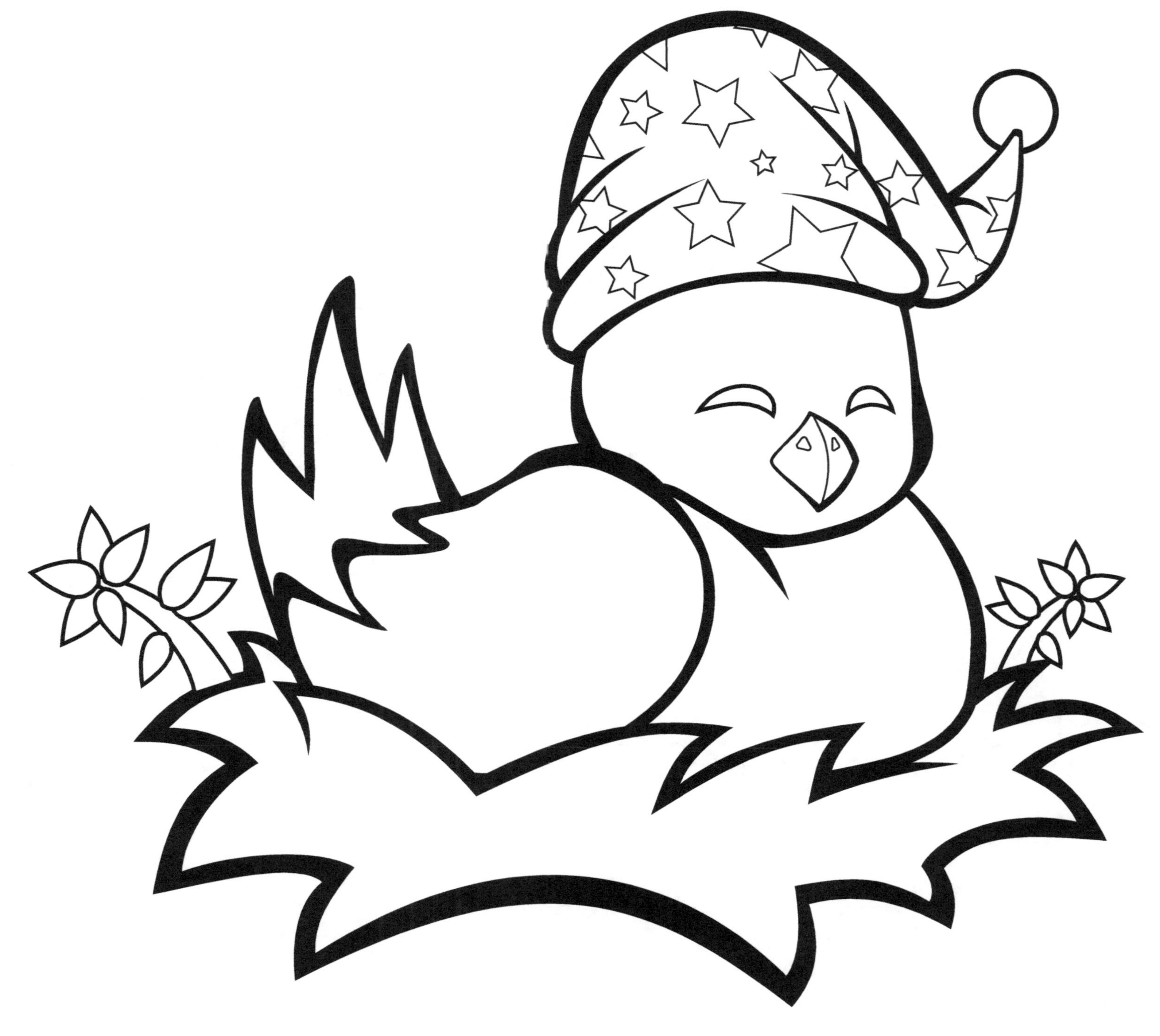

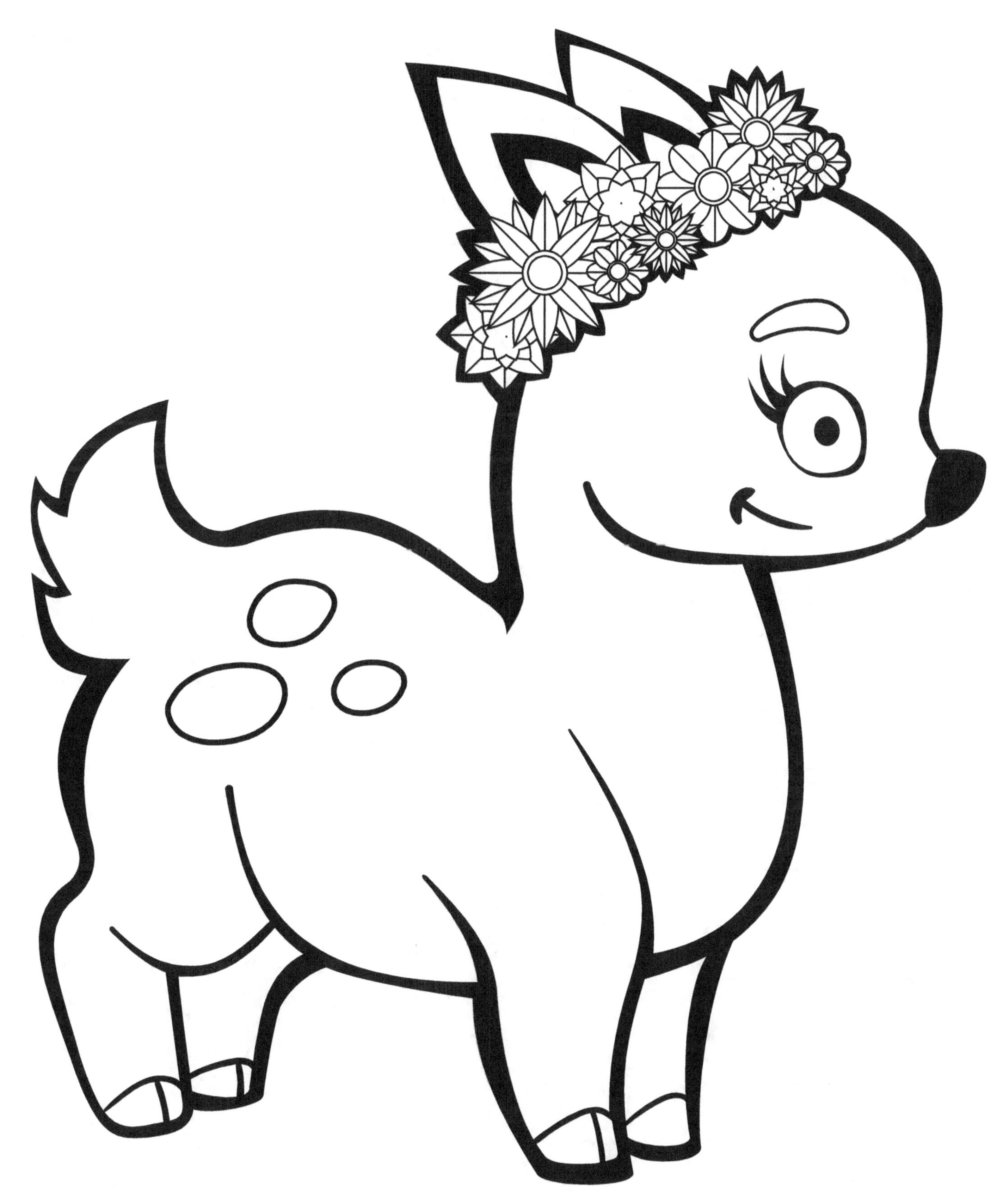

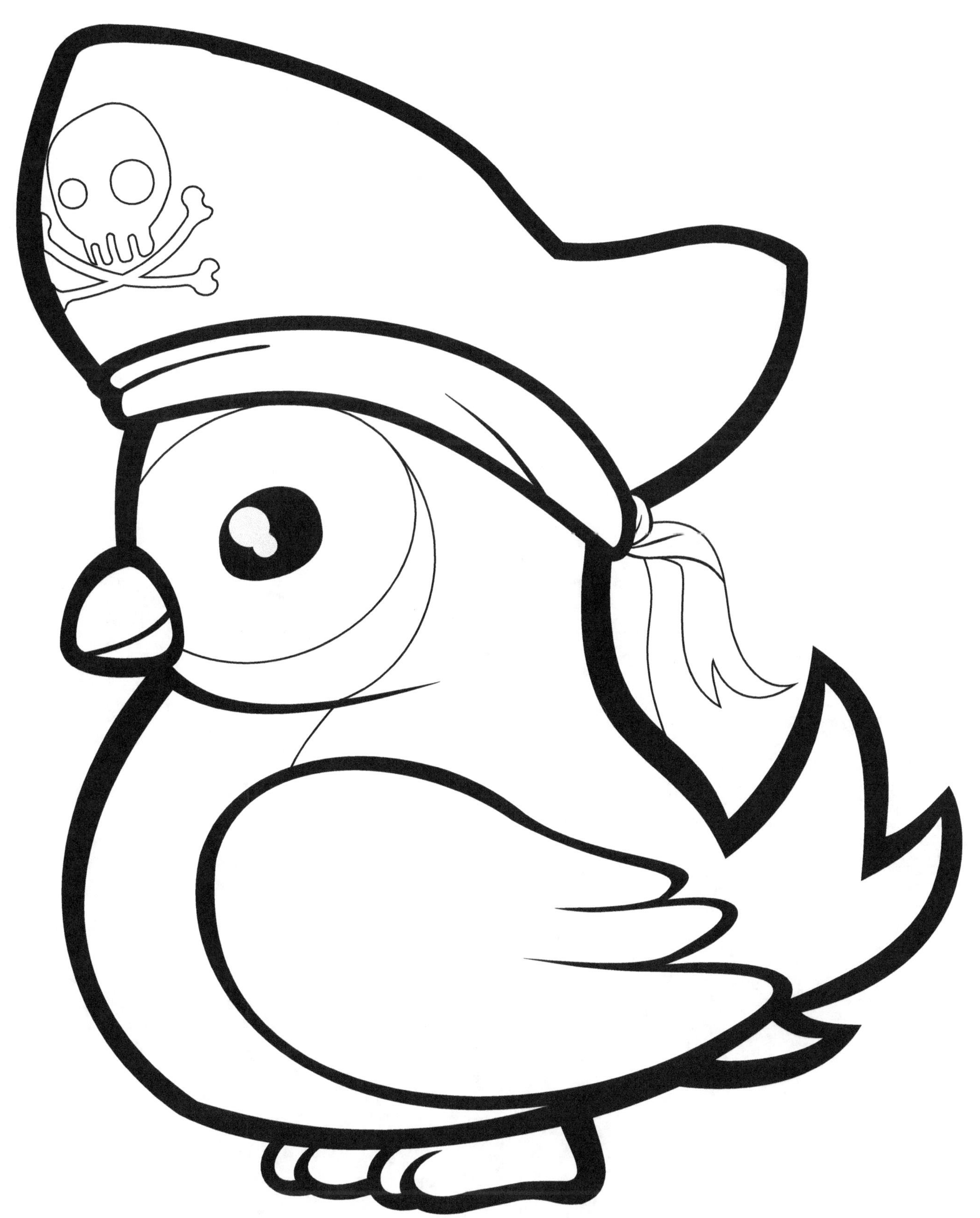

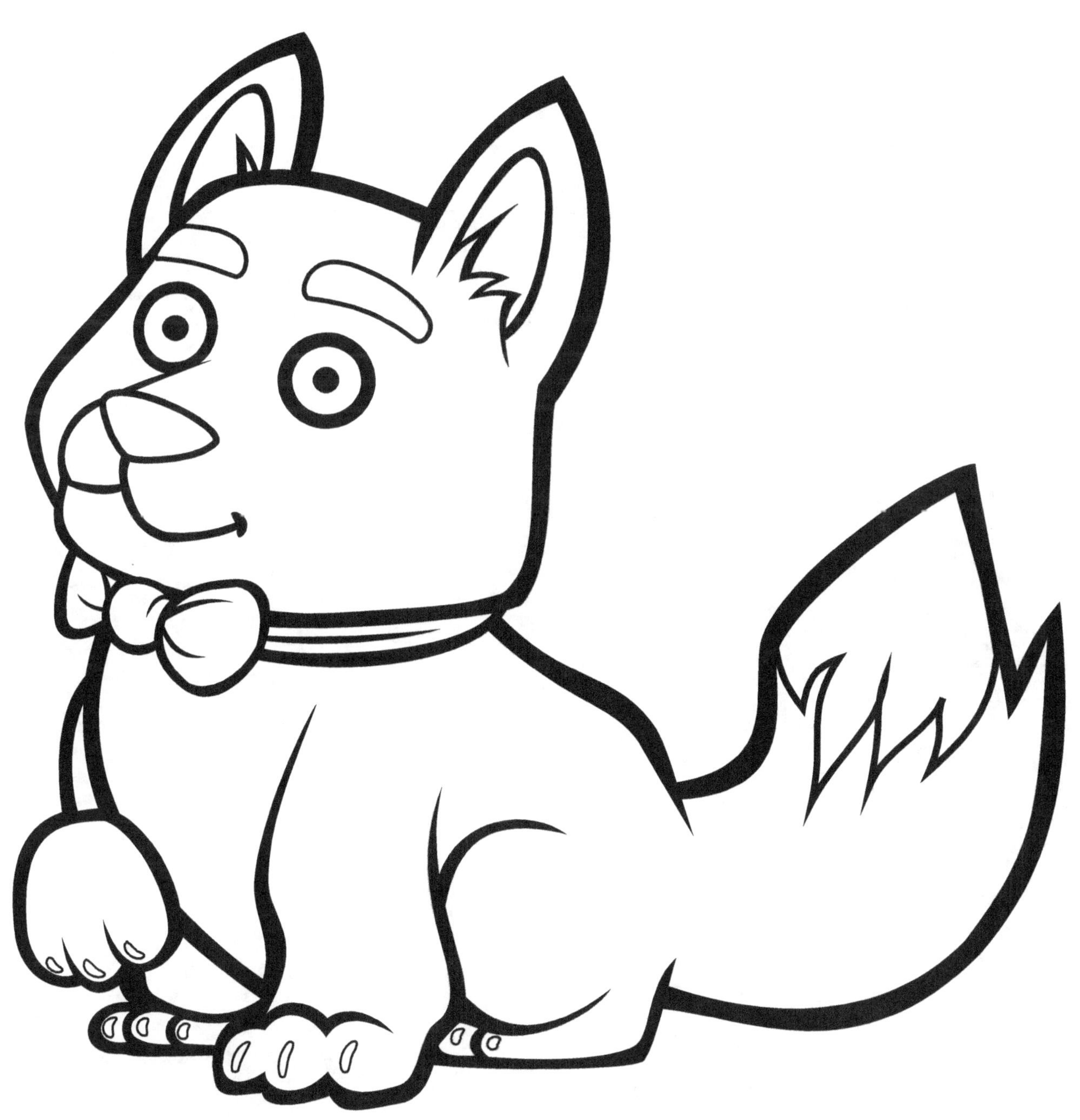

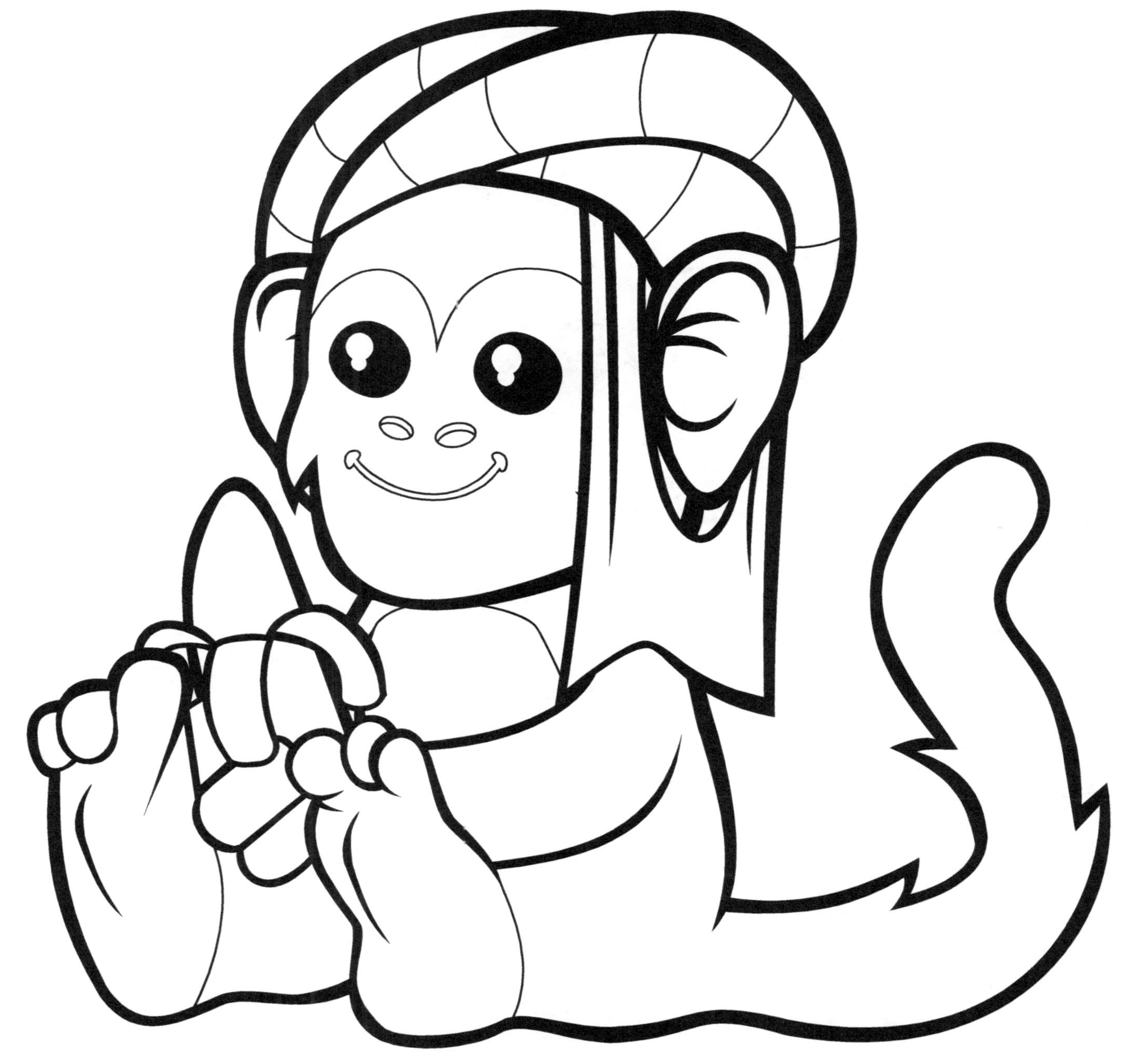

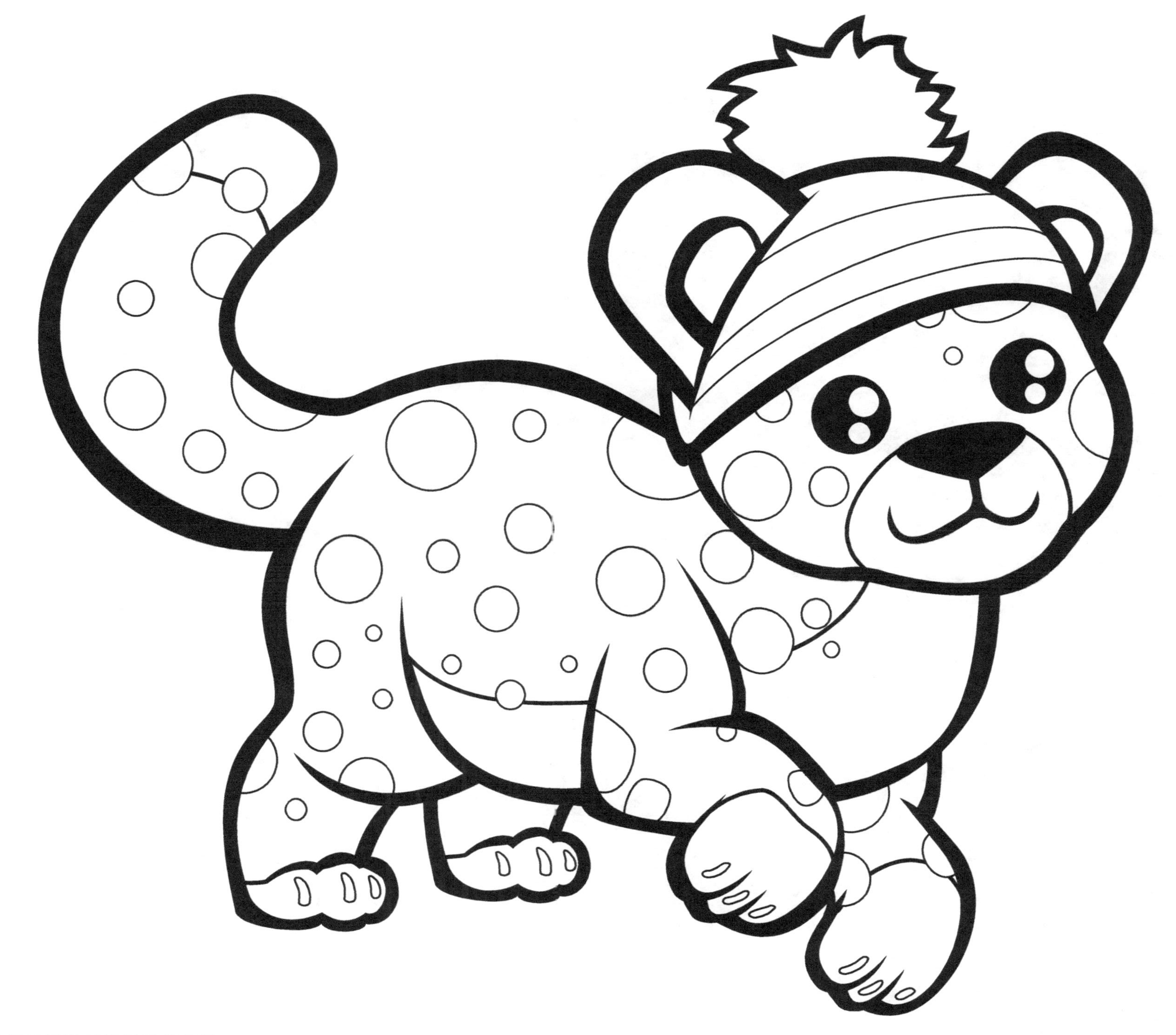

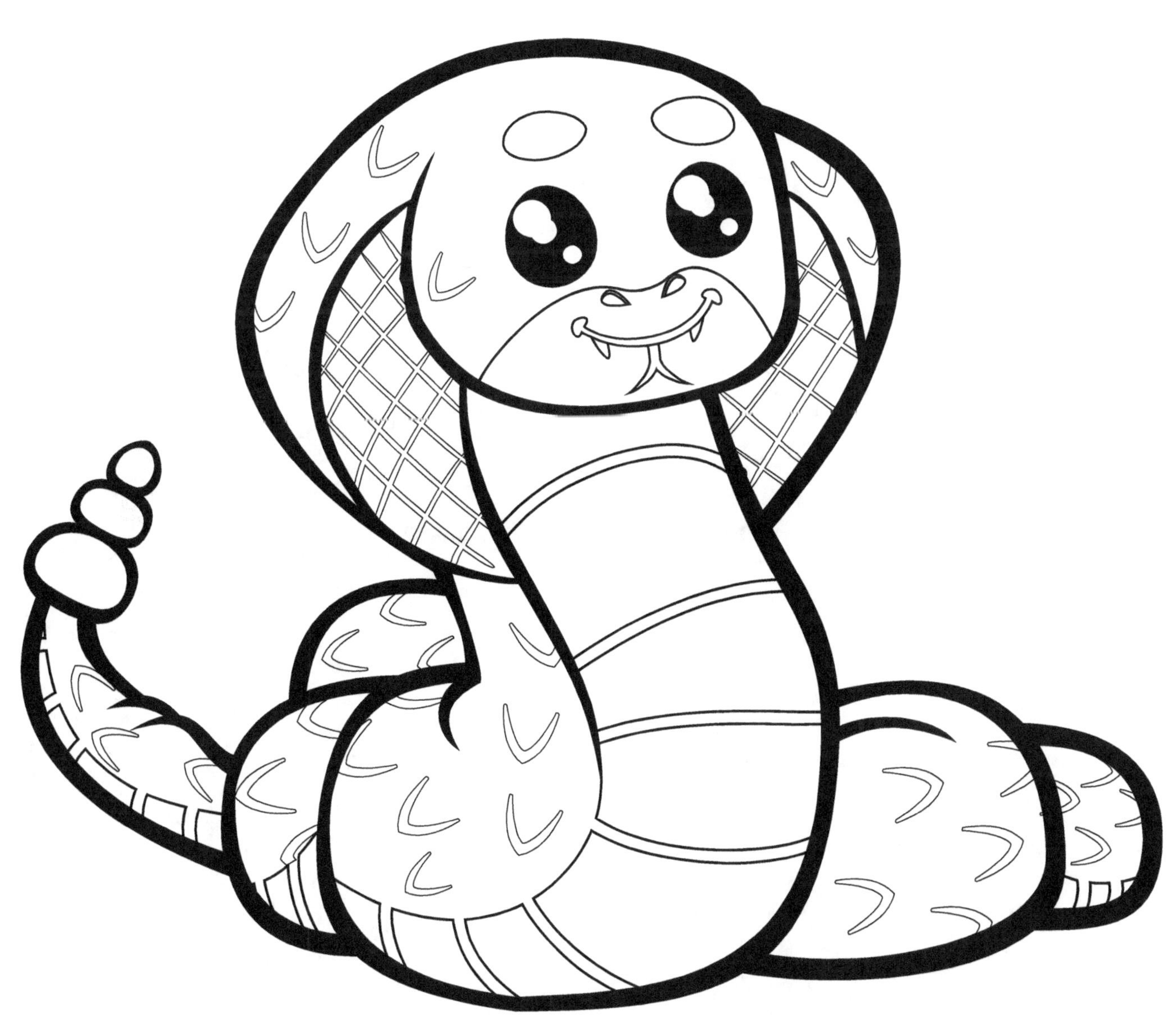

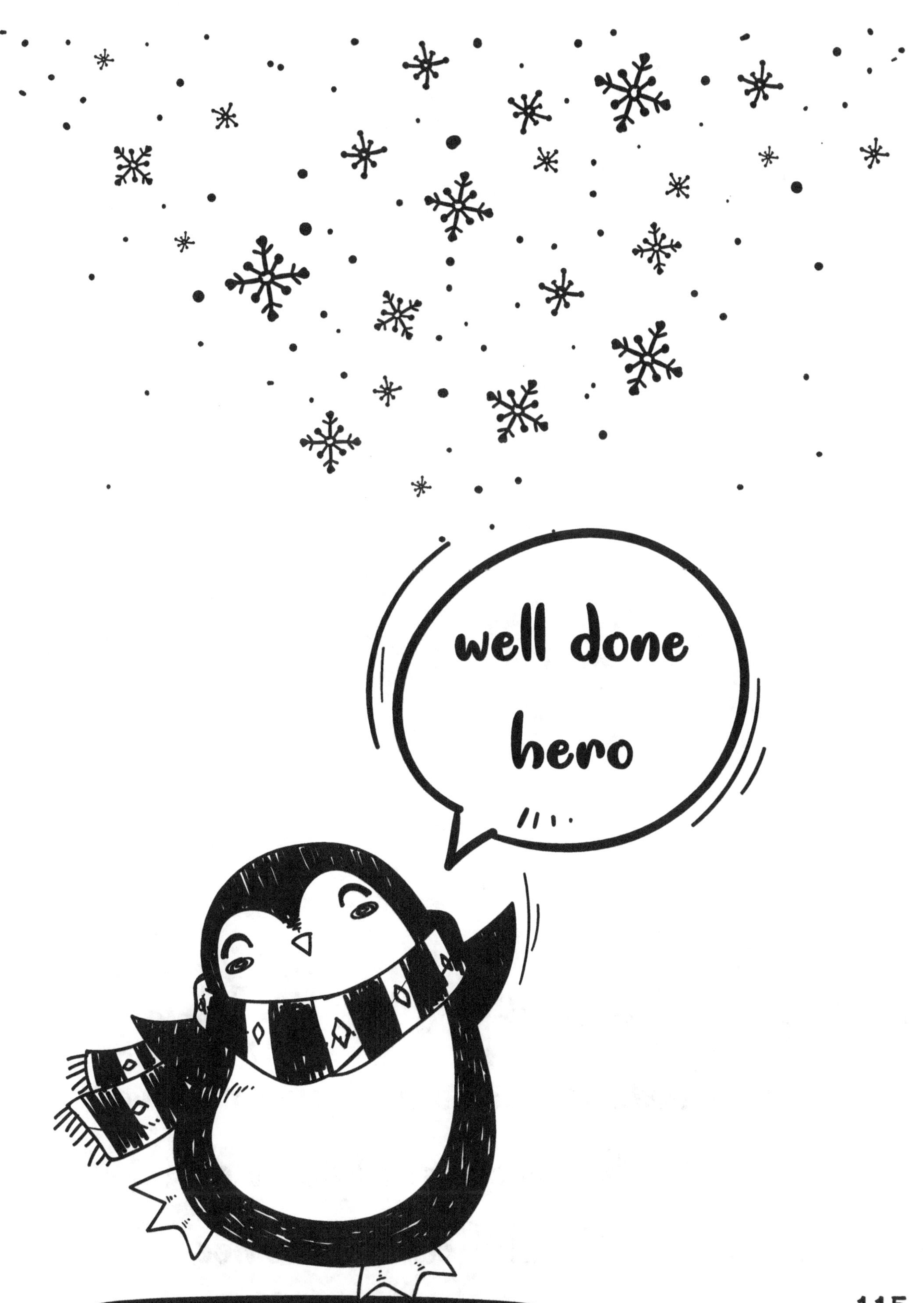

well done
hero

please if you like the book
rate it and leave your review
this means a lote to us
thank you in advance